Praise for Keren Dibbens-Wyatt and Garden of God's Heart

"I love reading Keren's work, she is a great writer." Richard Rohr OFM, Franciscan friar, internationally renowned writer and speaker, founder of the Center for Action and Contemplation.

"*Garden of God's Heart* offers a daily invitation into deep seeing of the world beneath its surfaces. I recommend this book as a dose of wonder each morning to spark a new aliveness in your heart."

---Christine Valters Paintner, PhD, author of ten books including her latest, *The Wisdom of the Body*

"*Garden of God's Heart* is at once lyrical and poetic, prayerful and metaphoric. Keren Dibbens-Wyatt's melodic and inspirational meditations evoke the spiritual sensitivity and sacredness of a bygone era. Her exquisite reflective images of the natural world combined with the author's pastoral prose, invite the reader to experience the blessing of daily reverie. This is a book to be savored and held within the heart.

Sibyl Dana Reynolds, author of *Ink and Honey* and *The Way of Belle Coeur*

Garden of God's Heart is a delightful collection of meditations from an English country garden. I love Keren's poetic prose which invites us into the contemplation of God's beautiful creation in fresh and insightful ways. Each phrase holds treasures of understanding that lingered on my tongue and in my thoughts, beckoning me to dig deeper and enter the garden of God's Heart. A refreshing and enjoyable book, not just for those who love gardens, but anyone whose senses are stirred by the fragrance of a flower or the beauty of a tree.

Christine Sine, author of *To Garden with God*, contemplative and gardener.

Garden of God's Heart

365 Meditations Inspired by the English Country Garden

Garden of God's Heart

Keren Dibbens-Wyatt

Migiwa Press

2017

First Edition 2017

ISBN: 978-1-326-93706-5

Copyright © Keren Dibbens-Wyatt 2017

Published by Migiwa Press
Contact for sales and all other enquiries: kerendibbenswyatt@gmail.com

Or visit our websites:

www.kerendibbenswyatt.com   www.stillwatersministries.co.uk

Dedication

This book is dedicated to the Good Gardener, and to all those who have helped root and establish me in his love.

With deep gratitude to:

My parents, Graham and Valerie, who planted me and continue to water me;

My brothers, Roger, Philip and Michael, who grew and grow with me;

Hugh and Ruth Dibbens who reflect God's light daily and inspire so many of the Lord's seedlings,

And especially to Rowan and Gareth, the canes that help hold me upright and the twine that binds me in loving embrace and keeps me close to the good earth.

Foreword

There are books that are beautifully written, books that tell great stories, books that contain deep spiritual truths and books which speak grace to the heart. Rarely is there is a book that does all these. This is such a book.

Images in both words and pictures have crept from the page into my mind, heart and spirit and taken rest and root there. Like the parables of Jesus where the simplest of stories contain heaven's treasures, so some of these devotional meditations have profoundly impacted me.

Keren paints with words and light and grace, deceptive simplicity that carries profound insight and opens new windows of understanding.

The Message Translation of Matthew 11:29 has Jesus saying, "Learn from Me the unforced rhythms of grace." I found this phrase so apt in summing up this exquisite devotional book. For me, it spoke to my heart of those "unforced rhythms of grace."

I hope you will love it as much as I do.

Jennifer Rees Larcombe

Author, speaker, counsellor, founder of Beauty From Ashes

Author's Preface

This set of devotions in poetic prose was written one day at a time, after spending a period of contemplative prayer with the image or reality of something wonderful on display (or, occasionally, lurking in the shadows) in an English country garden. It was a delight to find that even in my own tiny garden there were joys and surprises to discover and consider.

Each piece of creation, each flower, weed, fruit, insect, animal or raindrop, has something to offer those of us looking for lessons in life. Every fragment of soil has its own wisdom, its own share of the reflection of the divine in its life-giving nutrients and in the roots, worms and microbes that weave through it.

In praying our way through the wonders of God's gardens, we can, I discovered, learn more about his gracious heart; the heart that knew his human creations were happiest here, tending and co-gardening with the Lord, watching and living the cycles of the seasons and the comings and goings of all creatures great and small.

I hope you enjoy the delights and savour the sights of the Garden of God's Heart as it companions you through the days ahead.   Keren, February 2017

Acknowledgements

No writer is an island, so as well as my family I want to thank my friends for their prayerful support and encouragement. I'm not sure this book would exist without you.

In addition, I am always amazed at the generosity of photographers, both amateur and professional; and would like to thank everyone who has contributed pictures to illustrate this book alongside my own photographs. A massive thank you to Rowan Wyatt, Victoria Dibbens, Ged Cowburn, Kevin Thornhill, Jeannie Kendall, Chris Wicks, Dedo Mate-Kole Rampe, Jim Brown, Simon Roberts, Cathy Urquhart, Gill Fuller, Stephen Root and all the wonderful contributors at Morguefile and Pixabay who give their photographs for free to all of us creative folk to use. In a world obsessed with all it can get, such help for artists and writers given so kindly is a real blessing.

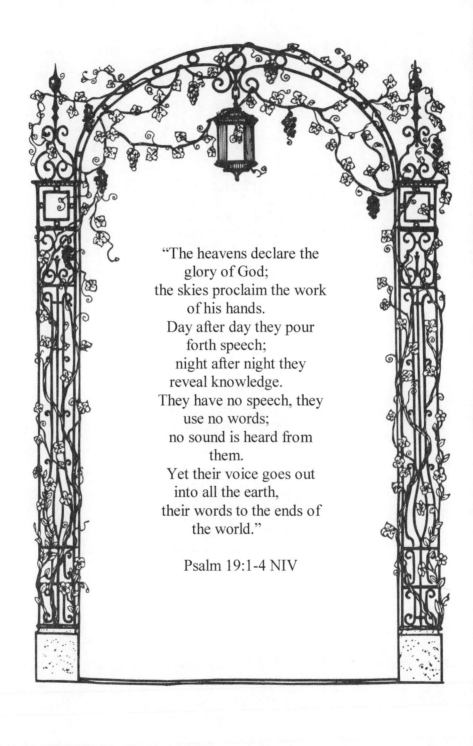

"The heavens declare the
glory of God;
the skies proclaim the work
of his hands.
Day after day they pour
forth speech;
night after night they
reveal knowledge.
They have no speech, they
use no words;
no sound is heard from
them.
Yet their voice goes out
into all the earth,
their words to the ends of
the world."

Psalm 19:1-4 NIV

Day One: Sunflower

Like the sun, God just keeps giving and giving and giving. The flow is unstoppable, unquenchable - fiery, holy goodness, love and blessings, words and wisdom – pouring forth the unfathomable, delicious knowledge of who he is.

Like solar panels, our angle is everything, determining if his light bounces off us or is absorbed. Let our faces then be set towards him like sunflowers, whose heads when budding follow golden glory all day and who then present that glory to the world like a face in a mirror, having gazed at his goodness.

Day Two: Clover

How we tread with such irreverence, trampling the Trinity in search of the aberration of four! Putting luck above love perhaps and seeking our fortune instead of seeing the green freshness of the triune family, each trefoil part-joined and whole at the same time, the chlorophyllic holy dance of unity played out before our very eyes.

Day Three: Growing in the Cracks

Starting small and pushing hard, working our way up and out into the light against odds where no wager could seemingly fail. Surely we began from a misplacing of seed from which we sought to free ourselves, in the end turning out to have been a holding in hardness and not a handicap, waiting until we were ready be unshelled and venture forth, green shoots blindly reaching, tendrils working against rock.

Taking then and now each day, hour, minute, fragile moment at a time, the desperation to thrive having been tempered by peace found in the deep dark learning curves we had to take, discovering solace in our difference and strength in roots and stems that took on concrete and won.

Day Four: Blossom

A canopy of palest pink, wrought in days, *Michael Angelo* heard weeping at the beauty that would grace any papal ceiling. Branches moving in the current of breeze like a tree-bound coral reef. Petals falling to cover the ground with a multitude of blessings over countless sin.

Perfect grace spiralling down like confetti marking the betrothal of spring and summer, a pact of joining. And must the blossom dance? Yes, or there will be no eating of fruit, nor a Fall to follow it. Prideful youth and beauty must be left behind, scattered on the earth like a sacrifice, so much green queuing up to take its place. Empires of pink must rise and fall so swiftly, like the *oohs* and *aahs* we breathe, called forth from our admiration.

Day Five: Daisy

Nothing daunts you it seems. Every day opening up to the world in hopeful expectation, each panel of your bridal gown bristling with hope, joined to your circle of gold in a wedded bliss of colour. A welcoming landing platform to any weary nectar seekers, open hearted like our Saviour to each leprous outcast. Drawing us in with your sunshine-centred greeting, a hoverfly's helipad. No thoughts for you of moving on, wondering where the grass is greenest; you stand your ground in joyful holding. An egg frying in delight in the heat of the day and the midst of the lawn. Your edges tinged with pink where the rays of setting sun caught you closing up shop.

We make you into chains, though you are far more connected than we know how to be. The lessons here for us, depressed and frantic, are too hard to learn, too simple to grasp. Nevertheless, your presence is a balm to our busy-ness and an antidote to our self-seeking days. *"Look up!"* you shout, *"Only look up!"*

Photo by Ged Cowburn, used with permission.

Day Six: Moss

Your softness turns a stone tempting to wield as a weapon into a pillow. You grow only in stillness and thrive in shadow. The master diviner, you teach us where to find living water, where to split the withholding rock and let it pour forth refreshing abundance.

Your feathered antennae bend in the breeze as though you were a squadron of resting moths, soon to take flight again. Your emerald lushness, velvet to the touch, speaks of a land we don't yet know, where the Lord of green pastures waits and speaks with gentleness.

Day Seven: Raindrops

Delightful dew-ish jewels, pausing a wee while on budding roses or lush green leaves to hold the light and dazzle us before you continue wending your way down into the dirt. Like our tears you travel onwards, pulled by the need to be collected. God's bottle, God's water table, places of pooling. Your pitter patter is soothing and cleansing, your freshness revitalising the dried-up surfaces and parched, thirsty ground.

Each ball of crystal holding the convex sky, each droplet refracting rainbow promises as it runs into another, beginning the joining journey that will end in oceans and clouds and rainy rebirth.

Day Eight: Tulip

So quick to appear in your brazen beauteous red velvet. Taking the green surrounds by scarlet storm, eager to proclaim spring and herald the sunshine. *"I'm here!"* You seem to cry, *"Stop everything!"* Our rain-weary eyes are drawn to your melodramatic presence. Even your deep dark false eyelash innards are mesmerising, outlined in gold and more suited to a queen bursting through Solomon's doors than to a plant sitting in a ceramic pot on my patio.

Egyptian treasure in a jar of clay, reminding us that the God of surprises lights up any corner of the world he chooses with stunning brightness, a glorious clammering for attention not, in the end, for yourself, nor the fields full of your sisters 'neath the windmill shadows of home, but pointing towards the one who stained you so deeply and made you the shouting of a bright *"Hallelujah!"* that echoes in our melted hearts.

Day Nine: Buds

So shy, wondering if it is safe to come out yet. Nervous of untimely frosty fingers and curious finch beaks. Yet come out you do, shrugging off mint green boleros, like satin-clad, delicate debutantes, small pink crinolined beginnings, looking around for advice on how to bloom with style, unsure of your perfection, not yet confident of your fruitful destiny.

Newly bare blushed shoulders feeling the breeze and the sun for the first time, blessed sign of spring and of things to come, all taking their place in the flowering queue. Such soft fragility, perfect confectionary colour, as if you were sugar mice unfolding your ears, making us feel sordidly old and world-weary, yet able to take solace in your frangible, delectable rose-kissed freshness. A quickening and a gladdening you bring to our tainted, fractured hearts.

Day Ten: Snail

Small spiral perfection, softly gliding unidextrously across the leaves. God's suction cup, holding foot-fast to every surface, leaving a trail of gloopy, loopy glittering across everything you touch. Your molluscular movements lulling us into a false idea of slowness, when in reality you cross gardens and climb trees with *Tarzan*ic ease.

The tears prick, each time I find a strimmer-shattered shell, or a thrush-hammered empty home. Your discarded gypsy caravans litter the garden like bitter disappointments and I long to collect and repair them all with glue and varnish even as I chide my own silliness and trace your abandoned curves with my fingers. But earthly means cannot refill a barren casing any more than they can rebirth faith long moved on. It is the Lord only who gives meaning to an empty tomb and raises despair transformed into a living and certain hope.

Day Eleven: Bumble

Tiger of the lilies, your fur coat seems unwieldy and hot for the courier work you are called to do, paniers of pollen loading you down. Fast food has nothing on you, frantically rushing from one nectar source to another, barely touching down before you are off again, *Rimsky-Korsakov*-ing your way helter-skelter to the next stop, like a Formula One racer roaring in and out of the pit. Yet perhaps time is entirely different seen through your compound eyes. Maybe you soar and float serenely from pink stage to yellow floor with balletic grace. Perhaps we see selfishly in your zooming, only our own harried busy-ness, reflected.

Day Twelve: Dandelion Clock

Is this the meaning of time hidden in your clock, then, that all things are eventually transformed? Your confident butter blonde locks shake into lion-toothed life, the Cornish ice-cream yellow mane gorging on sunshine, soon to shrink wrap itself in a green sepaled cocoon only to re-emerge as a crown of wisdom: your silver and fly-away hair a glorious grey afro that sends its knowledge out via dancing parachutes to be replanted wherever it finds fertile, willing earth. How can such a story of metamorphosis and generosity be a weed? No, I proclaim you an evangelist, a seed giver, a sender of your wisest, oldest self, given out upon the four winds to make disciples in every garden.

Day Thirteen: Bark

Old knotted skin, a layer of brown panelling protecting inner sap and softness, the deep crevices of armour plating on a wooden armadillo. Here we can trace the lines of your history, palm-istry and divination, but only of your past – seeing the hearts and arrows of long-dead love affairs and the scrapings and wounds from sharpened antlers, the fingernail crescents of hugs, dugouts of small feet climbing eagerly, eyes and knots and eerie faces carved by time and weather, your wounds becoming trophies somehow, like our wrinkles, each one hard earned, precious, costly, best worn with acceptance and humility. Ancient scars all now become story-telling, *Ent*ish poetry, taking its time and letting the rhythms of the deep rooted places rise up and take their place on the surface.

Day Fourteen: Lavender

Sweet, soft, heaven scent. A purple plushness of royal waves, as the wind bends you this way and then that; synchronised dancing, your goal to mesmerise us with movement and fragrance. On the breeze you remind us of gentle aunts and grandmothers long departed and of mild manners gone with them. Kind, listening ears that only whisper in the air even as they release their familiar "by *Yardley*" perfume. Gathered and lain by soft hands into trugs, by those who harvest only you and roses, for you will be touched by nothing indelicate. Dried and tied up with haberdasher's ribbon, you sing us to sleep from beneath our pillows and send us on to the land of Nod, or drip your oil softly into our bathtubs and soothe us with Lorelai lullabies, till we can let go at last and let dreams take us on.

Day Fifteen: Pigeons

Alighting with the grace of a thrown brick, then awkward and stumbling, edging out one precarious foot at a time along the slender branches that hold your roundness only by sheer determination (and a little faith). Pecking at the buds, your long necks reaching, Brontosaurus-like, down to the best and freshest morsels. Preening and stretching, your dappled greyness the perfect counterpoint to bursts of burnished bronze and purple collar caught now and again in the sunlight, proving that no creature is ordinary, and treasure always glimmers unexpectedly even in the most familiar of plumage.

Day Sixteen: Ladybird

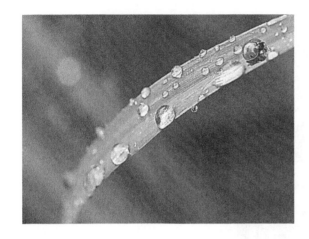

The scarlet and the black, your priestly cloak holds tight to cased layers of petticoat-wings, made of the finest dark lace. Your Catholic credentials borne further aloft by your association with Our Lady and the holy names you carry: our Good Lord's wee beastie (*lieveheersbeestje*), Moses' little cow, little messiah, Lady's bird. Wrapped in Mary's red cloak and decorated by her seven sorrows, you fall from a thorny crown of rose briars like a drop of blood shed for us.

A Cardinal, crimson carrier of insect incense, you waft cheerfully up and away like a hovering brooch; terror of the aphid, protector of the rose, defender of the faith, leopard of the garden skies, emblem of my early childhood reading, friendly-faced defier of fire in nursery rhymes, up, up and away you zoom, my imagination soaring with you.

Day Seventeen: Thorns

Spiky hurdles, difficult obstacles. Things that rip and shred and catch and get between us and the fragrance of roses. Could we have such a divine flower without your worldly reminders of pain? Perhaps your presence makes the costly scrapes still dearer.

Tearers and tormentors of precious flesh, emphasising the join between human and godly as you dig into the already bloody forehead. A crown of pain and deliverance, brought from three gardens: perfection, prayer and pain, the gardener's son hedged in here on this hellish hill by your circlet of mocking teeth. But the kingship your thicket bestows is not unwelcome, nor despised. It is the true revelation of His suffering, of what Love costs. And how should we know this without your sharp and piercing mountains, pointed reminders of our own ability to bleed and feel? Without you, the Rose of Sharon would seem less beautiful, less real, less whole, just as a red rose bred thornless would be like a divine word spoken from a toothless mouth.

Day Eighteen: Magpie

Bird of paradox. Black and white both together and separate, one seamless garment. The tension between sorrow and joy held in balance, murderous thoughts and love of treasure living together in your heart. Death and glinting swimming before your bright and deadly eyes simultaneously, your sight a lot like ours. Raucous call and glimmering plumage, awkward size and soaring grace. Like the spirit and the flesh, the human and divine, there is a tightrope walker here in the space between two worlds. An Easter Saturday clasping of yesterday and tomorrow that doesn't quite know what to feel or how not to fall apart from trying to cling to the centre.

Like Christ, who called you into existence, you hold the opposites beautifully, the horizontal and the perpendicular of the cross, reaching out across two planes, flying and walking, heaven and earth: a wingspan that spreads beyond our thoughts, as far as the east is from the west and then some.

Day Nineteen: White flowers

Small stars in the universe of grass, twinkling in the sunlight and covering the lawn with life, like a carpet of Tolkien's *Evermind*, a *simbelmynë* symbol of those gone before, the dead whose way you keep and whose memory we hold dear, the paschal flower of all-year round Easter eternity, the flower of remembrance, on hill and barrow. I wonder if you would flourish too, in the garden around an empty tomb, unfazed by roll-ed stone or angel's tread. White snowflake heads bobbing in worship to the greater fragrance of the returned, resurrected King.

Day Twenty: Hole in the ground

A mystery entrance, freshly dug soil the only evidence to convict you of trespass. Ants, bees, slowworm, fairy? I do not know. What you hold is the unseen, that cannot be discovered without spoiling your home, unearthing your burrow or turfing you out. Some secrets are best left undissected, the price of knowledge too high to pay. I will sit and wait then, like Mary Magdalene, keeping vigil in the garden, no stone here but only time to roll away. Keeping watch without sleeping is always hard where there is grass to lie on and shade to sit in and dreams to fall into.

Perhaps instead I will leave you in peace and not tower over your front porch, in case you are just inside, grave clothes neatly folded, face in a jar by the door, waiting for the all-clear to sound so you can come out and dance in privacy in the long, cool green at the bottom of the garden.

Day Twenty-One: Common Blue

Dainty, wing-ed flower, you flit in time with the unforced rhythms of grace from perch to blessed perch like a patch of blue summer sky come down to bring glad tidings of warmer climes. Such delicate loveliness we covet and long to catch, but you are so quick and ethereal we can barely hold you with a gaze or pin you down with a glance, before you are off again, thankfully escaping our envy, our hunger to keep you. Freedom, now so lost and ancient an art, is unfamiliar to us and the sight of you sparks off some deep, uncomfortable longing we would rather sidestep at the same time as it gives us joy. You may be small, but you are too much beauty to bear.

Day Twenty-Two: Buttercup

The holy grail of sheen and lustre, you hold your petals in a perfect round, like hands borne up in a circle of prayer. Lifting up a cry of *"Glory be!"* and a precious gift of fragrant air. You grace the fields and meadows and raise them to summer splendour, just by nodding your head of yellow joy. Your petalled church with all the people waving inside as they are moved by the breeze, just as we are by the divine breath. A solar hall of mirrors, pooling the dazzling sunlight, reflecting back and forth across your satin surfaces, so that the captured rays dance and bedazzle us. Who doesn't love butter when it shines and radiates so? A fairy crown of glister and green, clusters of hallelujah in every pasture. Real treasure, a field of gold worth selling up for.

Day Twenty-three: Nettles

Incorrigible, you grow with nerves of steel any- and every- where, strong and defiant, daring the foolish to grab you as if you were an ordinary weed and retreat regretfully stung. The bane of the gardener, friend of the butterfly, your caterpillar nursery offering shelter and nutrition to those who are hairy and green, just like you. Poking your head above every parapet, fast and furiously pushing your way with a comprehensive knowledge of your own rights, a political plant rebelling against whatever you've got, muscling its way into the rose garden, the arbour, the pergola, the shed, the marigold bed, ultimate trespasser and bringer of chaos, whose false belligerence is betrayed by delicate white or pale blue flowers, the befriending of creepy crawlies and the flavour of wild tea.

Day Twenty-four: Katydid (bush cricket)

An insect that looks like a leaf, green and fresh and deceptive. A reminder that compartmentalising God's work will always be met with the playful toss of a French sandal into the works. Classifying and carbon-dating foiled by a Cambrian shell in Cretaceous rock. The mysteries of symbiotic lichen, puffball fungi, duck-billed platypuses, aspen connected underground, ferns unchanged since the start of time, moss in suspended animation springing to life after an ice age, missing links and leaves with legs on.

Evolution, adaptation or creativity? Hers is a mind so vast it is in vain we try even to catch a glimmer of its nebulaic structure. Intelligent design that knows exactly how to break its own rules. He will not be held fast, made to fit our theorising, but instead slip through our fingers as we tighten our grasp, our attempts to dissect him ending as if we were clutching an ice cube in hopes of keeping it captive.

Day Twenty-Five: Birdbath

A truly Franciscan structure, an oasis in the garden, a place to pause, to bob and preen and flurry one's wings in a familiar rush of droplets; somewhere for the eagle in us to dive and be renewed, a refreshment for the next stage of the flight.

A comma in the day, a site for reflection in water and light, a breathing space, a long cool drink of satisfaction. An imbibing of life that runs down the gullet and the plumage in rivulets of rain. No tiresome drawing from a well here, but a collecting of heaven's provision in a basin of stone, ready for each wing-ed baptism; all recipients leaving with their ash shaken off, rising up in fiery streams of colour.

Day Twenty-Six: Blue Tit

A bubbly sing-song bird, bright and true, sky blue and sunshine yellow, your only hope of camouflage is high against a summer cloud. But who would hide such a treasure, a darling bud, a chirping, lively flitter between trees, between worlds? Heaven painted you with a lapis hood and cloak, and clothed you in a buttery jerkin, to bring cheer and loveliness to any dreary heart, and hope in goodness to any unbeliever.

Day Twenty-Seven: Wheelbarrow

Carrier of heavy loads, you wind your way around the garden path, legs held up in the air behind you, such a good sport, reminding us of childhood games. It is safe to lay our burdens on your shoulders, our yoke made easier by your willing balance. And when your working life is done, when all the cement and earth has worn you down and rubbed your wheel thin, and you are weary and old, then you can end your days resting by the wall, a planter for pink begonias, a retirement of red geraniums, a container for colourful chrysanthemums.

Day Twenty-Eight: Blackbird

Eyes like smoky quartz ringed with topaz, jewels set in the midnight of your plumage. A golden beak darting in search of treasure. Head to one side listening for the scurrying of spiders or the almost silent devourers of earth wriggling along under the surface of the world. Your friendly hopping gait endears you to all who watch.

Your song captivates the dawn and dusk, as well as the weary commuter who stops still on the corner to take in the recital. Eyes closed, heart open, the melody revives and encourages. There is hope still living amongst us, when such beauty fills the dull, commercial air.

Day Twenty-Nine: Dew

Waters rising up from the ground, droplets of morning, a coverlet of refreshment that charges even a skeletal leaf with new life. Held here and there in suspense, in fronds and webs and frames, like diamonds flung from an extravagant jeweller's hand, no expense spared even in the dishing out of gems that will soon evaporate in the warming rays of sun.

A blessing to accompany our daily bread, the manna water that is drawn up from the well of life, a raiment of nourishment and a pouring out of mercies that are fresh each and every day.

Day Thirty: Fledgling

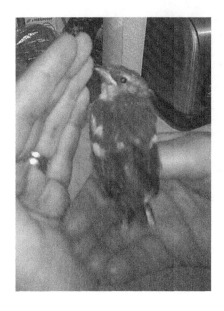

Far from home, fallen and bedraggled, the prodigal chick has a long road to recovery ahead of her. All that potential clear for us to see, unknown to you; your "L" plates bright, your unfamiliar wings and strange new feathers will guide you afore long, however odd they feel now. The rescue that feels like betrayal is a good thing, though your small unfocussed eyes are yet to see it. Soon the colours will deepen and your name will make sense and your gold will shine. Soon you'll see with bright eyes from high above that there is a different way to fall, and you will aim at the ground and miss, soaring away to freedom.

(Just so you know, this little lady is a goldfinch and she was found lying in the grass on the village green rather stunned, by our then foster dog, Lilly. We looked after her and then took her to the lovely folks at Folly Wildlife Rescue, who cared for her and released her into the wild when she was ready. She's a little out of focus in this photo but I think that's probably how she was feeling.)

Day Thirty-One: Sparrow

The moustachioed businessman of the garden, it would not surprise me to see you sporting a bowler hat and carrying a black umbrella under your wing as you head off to the feeder. Everywhere we go, you and your bib-less unbearded professional other half are there too, just as business-like, in eaves, in the park, by the roadside, darting to-and-fro.

No-one stops and stares, as they do with other birds, no-one remarks on your colours (glorious though they are) except to pronounce them plain. No-one puts you on the cover of a wildlife magazine or builds a hide to watch you. No-one places you in an ornamental cage or heaves dramatic sighs at your song. But your heavenly father sees every swoop and peck. He listens to every chirrup. And each one of you, worth half a penny to us, is his masterpiece, painted in pastel chalks and ochre browns, a symphony of flight and a source of pride and joy. Not quotidian to him, but each one as special as the next. No bird of paradise more worthy of his loving attention.

Day Thirty-Two: Bluebell

Flower Fairy hats in softest sheens, hanging your heads in the dappled sunshine, as if you are sleepy like me, and either just awakening, or in danger of nodding off. I fancy I hear a tinkling as the breeze blows and you gently shimmer. The epitome of prettiness, no wonder you've been welcomed here from your woodland beginnings, the corners of parks and gardens now awash with your carpets of deep sky.

To me, you mean so much, speaking of walks and wheelings with both earthly and heavenly fathers, and of my wedding day, where you rang out from around the churchyard, a campanologist's dream, and a sign of blessing on our union, our anniversary flower, and a burst of gentle joy every late springtime.

Day Thirty-Three: Cobweb

Captivating threads, a glistening death trap that mesmerises, like your architect's many eyes. Round and round she goes, never once glancing at the blueprint, feeding out sticky skeins. Holding flies and blossom, grasping seeds and supper, catching beads of gleaming in the gloaming and dust at dusk. All is treasure, accumulated, assessed, disposed of, sucked dry, the husks float like skulls on gate-posts, an unheeded warning to passers-by.

Beauty and danger, gossamer and glinting, surrender in silk. And then, when the web is torn and the lies fall away, all must be gathered in again, rolled up like a used parachute, eaten and respun, not made and mended but recycled and reborn: held, wound and joined so delicately by *Teflon* legs, the *Perspex* mandala reworked and ready once more, bristling in the breezes that carry the hunter's breakfast into your waiting gauze.

Day Thirty-Four: Caterpillar

Such a variety of outfits: furry coats, stripy vests, sleek green leotards, every fashion faux-pas you can dream of is worn with pride here. Warnings and camouflage, your only job is to defend your softness, your potential, what you will be more considered than what you are now, the idea of flight and beauty lying dormant in you, like a helicopter in Da Vinci's mind before he can scrabble around for a piece of parchment and something to draw with.

Munching machine, leaves left scarred and skeletal, covered in teeth marks or weighed down by your constant passing through. Traveller on the undersides, your stunning secret kept as close as your long, chambered heart. Fuelling up for transformation, just like us, knowing somehow you are not complete, unfulfilled and restless. Soon to sleep, perchance to change, becoming otherworldly and glorious, your journey through the cocooned valley giving us all resurrection hope.

Day Thirty-Five: Rhubarb

*Triffid*ic stalks and poisoned leaves, whoever thought to taste you first? Sharp and overpowering, your acid nature needs calming, stewing with sugar poured over you. Often we need such sweetness like balm to counter our own tongues, just as barbed and tart, something you will end up as companioned by custard.

Red and green, Christmas in May, a fruit or a vegetable? An identity crisis in the allotment, a sour sweet, a toxic treat, a leafy stem, a paradoxical pointer out of blurred edges and juxtaposed opposites, an oxymoron of a plant, then, made to make us question the more obvious crops in their ordinariness. Casual wonder thrown into the ground to grow more things than we can dream of in our earthly, mundane philosophies.

Day Thirty-Six: Vanilla

All that green, luscious growth and yet you are only prized for the tiny dusting of seed scraped from your bean-like clusters of pods that loll amongst your leaves like idle fingers bored of embroidery and lace-making. A delicate flavour shall be your handiwork instead, black treasure hidden in long chambers; mixed into ice cream, pressed into essence, magically changing milk to custard and adding spice to cake.

By rights so exotic, only grown here in Kew, yet you made the mistake of allowing yourself to become popular and then quotidian, so your taste is now deemed ordinary and plain, the base for some less familiar coolie or unheard of sensation. Yet how we would miss you, if you were no longer in the cupboard, in the freezer, in the cornet, in the cakes! A staple, kitchen standard, cook's friend, no humble plant you, but an orchid, lovely and surprising, most welcome tropical addition to our lives.

Day Thirty-Seven: Rainbow

A promise ribbon falling in a cascade of colours through the air as the sky dries its tears and finally lets the sun shine. A bridge between sadness and joy, arcing across the divide between creation and re-creation. Your partialness just as much an illusion as your sudden appearance, when of course your spectrum is always there and you are just one visible section of God's wedding band, round and perfect, a sign of covenant grace encircling those he loves, people and animals, to whom he says, *"Never again,"* and *"I am with you always."*

Hovering hues, high and holy, a sneak preview of the kingdom to come, like a glimpse of God's petticoat sweeping through the blue. A breakthrough of that world to this. An eternal beau of brightness, almost unbearable in its simple vibrancy, so that it must depart into the invisible soon and fade. Those who have eyes to see, let them see.

Day Thirty-Eight: Azalea

Like an alien
welcomed onto
English Victorian soil
where most foreigners
were spurned, your
exotic blooms made
their home here in the
grey and green,

shivering despite wearing your bright, crinkle-edged shawls. Whenever I turn a

garden path and see you I am back at *Manderley* again, down by the Cornish

shore, on high, blustery pathways looking out to Smugglers' Bay, feeling

mysterious and windswept.

Your Eastern hues confound us; saffron and amethyst, spice and depth that

intoxicate and cheer those of us used to smaller, more subtle (more Anglican)

displays of glory. We are learning to see this is not ostentation, but your own

natural way, free from artfulness, not tightlipped or anxious like us, but careless,

unconscious self-abandonment, true liberty despite edging a rectangle of

manicured green; caged and domesticated, but free in your colour-saturated

vivacity.

Day Thirty-Nine: New Growth

Savaged by the not-so-careful hand of fate, you found a different tangent for growth, a course correction, a side road, unseen before, at right-angles to the well-trodden path. Here you find that despite the worst life can do to you, hope does indeed spring eternal, and no-one is more surprised than you, in your green freshness and budding joy.

You still carry your battle marks and always will, but now you know that wounds become trophies, scars become stories, all becomes priceless wisdom. Without the chainsaw there would be no resurrection bouquet, without the *stigmata* there would be no witness, and we would not see that everything ordinary has an extraordinary tale to tell, every injury a depth to bear and an ability to bring forth fruit.

Day Forty: Cat

Monochrome loveliness of a fence-balancing, shed-walking, tree-climbing gamboler. Small furry welcome with delicate meowing hello. Tail wrapping food-wrangler, champion gaze-holder, chaser through tunnels of toys, bells and catnip. Stress busting softness, disperser of angst, guzzler of epic proportions and flattener of grass, sun-spot diviner and melter of hearts.

(for those who wish to know, this is our beloved cat Melody, who, despite her name, detests music and does not sing very well.)

Day Forty-One: Lady's Slipper

Golden velvet fit for Cinderella's danced out feet, though you do not come in pairs. Such soft material must tempt the cobbler elves from their hiding places and have them stitching surreptitiously through the night. Meadow flower, such joy to have your treasure winding through my lawn and poking your butter-coloured Cerberus heads up into the light.

Day Forty-Two: Anemone

Purple perfection, a parasol blown inside out by a staunch breeze. Your silken petals dance and rustle, overlapping and jostling like a meeting of suffragettes, the mauve, white and green all singing loudly here.

I can feel a hymn of independence brewing in your veins, and I see how the strong stalk helps you hold your Jodrell Bank head up high in hopes of catching the first rays of spring sunshine. To me, you will always mean the gift of creativity, lost for so long and re-given in grace, a remembering of my godmother Gwen's still life painting, reanimating my hopes of making something good, something to lift a day or start a smile at the corner of a sullen mouth; something to begin a thought at the edge of a blossoming mind.

Photograph by R.R. Wyatt, used with permission.

Day Forty-three: Dovecote

The peace penthouse, several stories tall and full of scattered seed and the purest white: feathers; droppings and the softness of snowy plumage. A signpost for truce, the olive branches all make their way here, and the flights to take them to the desperate, outreaching hands all begin in these archways. For Miss Jane, airing the schoolroom, a mark of gift, of family, of a new beginning, stable and true.

Day Forty-Four: Starling

It was in reading about you that I first tripped over the word gregarious, and a love of words and birds was swiftly born. Flocking together you are feathered friends of a different colour scheme: peacock green, emperor purple and royal blue; mottled cloak and bright beak; you own as much of the rainbow in the right light as any of your tropical cousins, and yet in shadow you can slip away like an assassin.

Your murmurations are mesmerising, swooping in synchronised elegance, a display of vortexing waves, dancing divers, a stirring of the skies, a symphony of movement, an aurora borealis of black balletic shapes, an ornithological wonder of the world.

Day Forty-Five: Cuckoo Spit

As a small child I imagined you propelled from an angry bird, back before they fired missiles at pigs. Maybe one held in the crook of a ventriloquist's arm, like a blue Emu, only smaller, spouting its saliva all over the garden. Tiny tots take things literally.

Now I know you are a nymph nursery, a playpen for baby froghoppers, a couching, frothy cloud to hide away in, keep warm and moist in. A haze of bubbles to confuse and insulate. A mantle, a haven, until the young are grown and able to jump away from their enemies. How we all need such protection, such covering, such snowy spittled cloaking, till we can learn which way to leap and how high!

Day Forty-Six: Garden Gate

Creaking in the wind, your boundary is a small thing, a deterrent or a welcome, a

stalling so we can look out of the butler's pantry window and see who

approaches, friend or foe. Posties abandoning all hope if they hear barking,

visitors smiling as they pass a pot plant to their other hand to reach for the latch,

politicians fearless and undaunted. Ineffectual your guarding may be, but

faithful, honest and reassuring, like a swinging sentry box or a border control

barrier. Here is a home, you say, and here is a fencing: in and out, *en guard*, be

clear whose side you are on.

Day Forty-Seven: Red Admiral

Flying the flag, you unfurl yourself across the summer sky, bright and glorious. Nautical manoeuvres of the first order, uniform to suit your rank, and the air waves are ridden in sumptuous majesty by your ship, sails clipping the wind and gathering speed.

Black as an eclipse, red as blood, white as wool washed clean, here you live out your short garden days reminding us of true sacrifice, of freedom won and souls that soar on colourful, hard-won wings.

Day Forty-Eight: Stones

 Smooth, flat, round, like the world before Hildegard and Eratosthenes, more comprehensible and easier to hold in mind and hand than Columbus' "New World". Chalky and white, how can such fossilised sea-skeletons have ended up here, risen to the soil of this hilly, fenced off place? Only a stopping point on a journey of aeons no doubt, a few moments of being a table for the thrush to smash snail shells on before moving off as the valleys are raised up and the mountains are levelled and all the layers of ages are pushed and pressed and remade.

Our new names shall be etched upon such as these, and our hearts changed from stone to flesh in response. With ice ages, receding forests and volcanic seas written in your veins, no wonder you are the apposite gift for an overcomer.

Day Forty-Nine: Saxifraga

Not content with one shade of pink you embrace them all, some heads angled into shadow take on deep cerise and other faces stare at the sun in apple-blossom,

ethereal paleness. You cover the ground in mossy chervil green and open your cheerful parasols gently towards the spring light in a composition of colours that would make Monet weep.

Soft and silken, yet known as *Rockfoil* and *Stonebreaker*, you hold medicinal properties and strong noble names dear and easy in your delicate being. Rosy treasure in the herbaceous border, singing songs of healing and harmony, a picture of pink perfection.

Photograph by R.R.Wyatt, used with permission.

Day Fifty: Pansy

From small and delicate wild *heartsease* you come, bred large and blood bright or royal purple and butter yellow for our viewing pleasure. Still an easer of hearts and a sight for sorely bored eyes. Your smile lights up the day and your little panda faces streaked with mascara brighten the border, the window box, the pot on the patio, the children's garden.

Thoughts begin in the heart sometimes and pensees, *"...pansies, that's for thoughts"* are held tight in Ophelia's bouquet, to soon be strewn about as she and her thinking begin to wander into water and fade into darkness. But held still longer, perhaps you could have eased her troubled mind and soothed her shattered heart, as gazing on you once did for me.

Day Fifty-One: Ants

No rubber tree plants to carry off here, but underground metropolises to build and hills to cement and walls to tunnel into. Colonies of busy-ness, your co-operation and efficiency put the Swiss to shame and their clockwork too, no doubt. Do you ever stop and smell the flowers, or savour the water drop you roll, or sample the leaf you carry? Or is time your enemy, the hours going by too fast with too little accomplished, as you rush about your complexes and organise your childcare and work all the minutes God sends? Are you more like us than we know, farming aphids and running nurseries and digging through mountains because they are there?

Day Fifty-Two: Chaffinch

God's mixing palette, a dab or swirl of so many different colours, you sing and

work your sturdy beak on buds and seeds. Strong-voiced and striped, your grey-

blue hood no disguise, we see you briefly, hopping fences like the un-

opinionated, ducking and diving, nature's spivs, keeping to the shadows and

coming out, *Walker*-like, to show your painted goods in your cockney glory.

Photograph by Kevin Thornhill, used with permission.

Day Fifty-Three: Compost Heap

Freshly shorn mowings and carelessly thrown peel, weeds and tares, shells and husks, potplants that did not respond to green fingers: all end up here in a *gehenna* of the lost and discarded, incubating rotten eggs and banana skins and the beheadings of roses.

Heat and compression for the unwanted, which, like the earth, is warmest at the core and home to unexpected swarms of life. Waste not wanted, nor wasted, forming food for flowers and decomposing into the nutrients that will sustain and nourish new beginnings. Majestic mulch, rich rubbish, like common carbon turned by pressure and warmth into something priceless. Heaven's here, performing its specialty, the total transformation of the lost and the cast out.

Day Fifty-Four: Rose

As *Dusky Maiden* and *Irish Eyes* know, you still smell as sweet by their names.
Layers of silken petticoats, a crinoline of rustling beauty, white as a '99, red as
Blake's love, orange as a hothouse apricot, yellow as late summer sun, pink as
Penelope's Rolls. How we love your hybrid loveliness, your shrubs, your game
climbing of trellises in skirts, the somehow perfect paradox of softness and
thorns.

Our Rose of Sharon took on the thorny crown and the gentleness of petals. The
whip of cords and the healing touch. All here for the knowing in an English
country garden, his fragrance waiting to be discovered by any passer-by with the
time and humility to stoop.

Day Fifty-Five: Shield Bug

Armour-plated you brave fiery arrows and darting beaks, becoming still and leaf-like to fool our feathered friends. Fearlessly laying bright green eggs and marching up rose stems, taking off into the blue beyond, *Buzz*-like and confident that your guardian wings will see you through. You seem like a tiny superhero, and I wonder how hard it is to put on six-legged tights. You take me back to petrol stations in childhood, books of *Green Shield* stamps being passed across the counter by my father, my confidence in him boundless; my shield, my illustration, the starting to see, of the father I would come to know, the defender of the weak and powerless, under whose wings I am shielded now as then.

Day Fifty-Six: Hawthorn

Hanging over the fence from the pathway beyond, not strictly part of the garden but claimed by your reaching arms, heavy and leaning now with white May flowers. Still drizzly here and with grey oppressive skies, no clout has yet been cast. Perhaps the weight of the clouds will fall along with your petals, like a freeing striptease, casting your satin veils into the warmer wind.

You remind me of hedgerows and country lanes and muddy boots. Of your shadow hanging over shy summer flowers and your red berries brightening every winter walk. For now, the green and white reign in long swathes, at the edges and the meetings of paths. A stalwart of our rural lives and their intersections.

Day Fifty-Seven: Nest

Here in the gutter or in the eaves, in the top of the cherry tree, away in the distant monkey puzzle, there are homes now built, some steady and sheltered, some swaying as if atop rigging. All being filled or being flown. Surplus moss is thrown down and sinewy twigs gathered up and woven; mud, hair and hay used as draught excluders, thatch and daub.

Each home a castle, each rough circle an opportunity to hold life, to nurture and continue exhaling the breath of God. Every grasping, hollering beak a chance at taking on the challenge set before us, to enclose and protect, endure and husband, every help we give a choice to tend, and love the career that was always set before us, from the very first, to garden.

Day Fifty-Eight: Aphids

Garden cattle, you roam the rosy plains and bug the buds, free and abundant, like green and pink dots on spindly stilts. Food for ladybirds, milking for ants, woolly miniature sheep, we are supposed to spray you with indifferent hatred, but my loathing of chemicals and love of life is too strong now.

How you speckle all the greenery and turn each flower into an impressionist's vision. Moving pixels, tiny devourers, small sherpas making always for the tips and the tops, looking down on the world from your high pastures, unaware of your villainy.

Day Fifty-Nine: Philadelphus

Sweet scent luring moths in the dusk, summertime fragrance that wafts heavily across the garden. Purest white and lily-like blooms, pouring out mock orange aroma that floats fruitiness all around.

A *perfumier*'s midsummer night's dream and an oppressive opiate of olfactory sensations, your weighty sugar drifts up and over, down and through, just as your tendril stems intertwine with other shrubs, as though you were placing your flowers in their hair, making elven mischief that *Puck*-like, winds its way through the garden.

Day Sixty: Goose Grass

Sticking to our school jumpers like Harold Lloyd's balloon, you were hooked

into the wool and knitted into our childhood as we looked over our shoulders and

tried to remove you as our friends giggled. Nature's *Velcro*, clambering and

grabbing onto anything and everything, your mini football seeds just as

fascinating, those little pellets that stuck more surely than the ones we threw at

our furry dartboard game. Clumps of them hanging here and there, congregating

in strange places like meetings of tiny aliens, cleaving to anything blindly, like

an unthinking bride and groom.

Day Sixty-One: Song Thrush

Accomplished maestro of the art of the voice, precious warbling throat full of airs and arias, you pitch your stage regardless of audience, and sing with your eyes shut to adulation, open to the skies.

Your Thor-like tendencies and expertise with an anvil are a less soft sound, your snail shell hammering a far cry from the delicate *obligatos* of dawn and dusk. Your knock opens secret doors, not just on dwarfish *Durin's Day*, but with every ray of starlight straining across the universe to hear the song of a dappled daydreamer.

Day Sixty-Two: Eggs

A clustering hexagon of mystery, alien pods with who knows what new life form within, unfolding and gestating, baby bugs being knitted together by unseen hands. Every underside of a leaf or stalk a possible hidden nursery. I check on you each day, waiting to see what will appear.

When you break out of your tiny world, from strait-jacketed embryo into "*a spacious place free from restriction*," I wonder if you are startled or dazed as I would be to finally have my boundaries broken down, my shell shattered and my time come, or if you just pootle merrily along, knowing and living happily in your bugginess, true to yourself and not imagining that there is anything miraculous about transition as you venture forth with fresh legs and untried wings.

Day Sixty-Three: Peony

Unfolding gradually from a marbled hard-boiled sweet, strawberries and cream, you slowly unfurl and free your many petticoats. You shake your bobbing heads and each day they bend lower, though whether with the heaviness of cares or the weight of beauty, is not for us to know.

Petals collected as they fall, as if they were precious teardrops, and kept carefully to fall once more over newlyweds, the best natural confetti, large tender hearts that rain down twice, in loss and then love.

Day Sixty-Four: Goldfinch

Swooping and flitting together you are a charm, though we call you a nugget instead, a bright perfect treasure, serendipity of colours, like heaven's flag or Aslan's colours, waving in dips and bursts across the sky. Trilling your song and alighting in the tops of the thinnest, bending branches, not minding the squallish summer winds or the impish breezes, your claws holding tight and your equilibrium more than a match for the best pirate, sporting your crimson balaclavas and taking your pieces of eight from feeder to feeder, thistle to thistle, treating us all to a display of doubloons.

Photograph by Kevin Thornhill, used with permission.

Day Sixty-Five: Sundial

Standing stone, you see the weather pass as Meister Eckhart did, knowing your clock remains the same whether clouded or wet, soaked in sun or touched by starlight. The time is reliable and never doubted, whether you can show it or not.

Stillness is mastered here and the art of contemplation studied as your one hand stays constant and the sun casts its shadow on your face, moving around you as we once thought it did for us. Segmenting time, measuring hours by presence, silent and immovable as the mountains from which you are hewn.

Day Sixty-Six: Fence

Boundary that brings security and a sense of ownership, though our time here is minute and our grasping illusory. Better to hold things lightly and know it is good to have edges and limits, given our tendency to roam beyond our borders into places that are full of the lost.

Home is best, and his dwelling places here are less obvious to our eyes, but we are his earthly courtyards and her mystery finds a hearth within our souls. Fenced in, hedged in, by bounds and barriers, we thank heaven for restraints and delineations that keep us sane and ordered and lived in. We do not have the capacity for infinity yet, and must keep to our properties; blessed by palisades and pickets, by the overlap of wood, the weaving of chicken wire and the warning of barbs.

Day Sixty-Seven: Onion

Bringer of tears, stinger of eyes, a rooting, shooting vegetable. Silken strands that peel, green life that springs up and away, all wrapped up in crinkly brown paper. Acidic sweetness, flavour that no chef can do without, garlic's cousin, scallion's sister.

Like a model of ego, your layers peel off, one by one, I must decrease, he must increase, gradually getting nearer to the core, to the centre, stripping away the desires till we are left with the ones that matter, right at the tear-shaped heart.

Day Sixty-Eight: Slug

Homeless snail, squelchy scavenger, you slurp your way around the garden and chew your path through the flower beds and the vegetable patch. Motoring mollusc, you ditched the caravan of your Romany cousins, swapping shelter for speed just like Mr Toad.

Here on the patio I can see that the rainy night brought you and your friends out to dance, making an ice rink out of concrete; the marks of your slow motion *Bolero* glistening in the morning sun. All day you will be dreaming up more schemes for tangos and triple *Salkos* whilst devouring cabbage leaves, no doubt.

Day Sixty-Nine: Mown Grass

Cut down in your prime yet releasing the freshest fragrance I know. A blessing rising into the nostrils that comes from sacrifice and death, you laying down, giving up your choicest green. A picture of resurrection too, knowing your roots are not cut off and you will rise again, ascending, growing up into the garden air. Even your cuttings will foster new life as compost or feeding hay, set before rabbits or mulching 'round flowers. His story of transformation is everywhere, even spread out before us here, in the life cycle of my lawn. Precious, so precious, these eyes to see.

Day Seventy: Sap

Oozing, not like blood from a wound, but the healing honey that forms a scab,

the balm of Gilead gently covering your pruned places and your injured limbs.

The scar left here will be transformed with a layer of amber, and patiently, oh so

slowly the golden barely-fluid will soothe the exposed and weeping hurt with its

own kind of mellifluous molasses and make the brokenness beautiful.

Day Seventy-One: Basil

You put the herb in our herbaceous borders and the pesto in our pasta. Such perfect green oval leaves, which bring smooth grace to our dishes and fresh fragrance to our nostrils. A healthy breathing in of Tuscan tavernas and an evocation of plazas we've never even seen.

A smile always creeping up on us too, as we remember a black and white deerstalker, a red Austin estate being birched to within an inch of its life, and a small, cheeky fox bending in raucous laughter. Yes, we will put you in the *ratatouille*, dear friend.

Day Seventy-Two: Forget-me-nots

Like standing stones on hilltops, you are there to keep memories. Like the knots in granddad's hanky, there you softly stay; not shouting, not nagging, just a present reminder of things that must not be forgot. First loves and first kisses, last landings and last goodbyes, sister to the poppy in the reminders you keep, yours soft and blissful, maybe, perhaps bittersweet sometimes: promises made under shady trees, only the worn carved heart and the small blue flowers bearing witness, holding you to your long-since-broken word. Soft periwinkle sky souvenirs, waving in the wind, whispering, "*Never forget, never forget,*" not as a condemnation, but so that none of the story gets left behind or lost. Tales are fragile like that.

Day Seventy-Three: Steps

Insurmountable tiers on bad days, helpful stationary escalator on others. *Steppes* built into the slope of a hilly, wind beaten garden. Old stone and grassy tufts, hidey holes for spiders and woodlice, homes that agoraphobic millipedes run quickly to and from, keeping close to the rocky edges, tiny hearts beating, fearful of open green spaces and giant, hungry beaks.

Ups and downs, there and back again, a concrete ladder for reaching other levels, finding and holding onto elsewhere blessings that come from the struggle of grabbing on to the handrail, keeping going, gritting our teeth and climbing, leaving us limping maybe, but well-travelled and wiser.

Day Seventy-Four: Harlequin

American invader, over here, eating our aphids, a negative of our own ladies,

colours surprisingly reversed, showing us the modern way of doing things. A real

jitterbug, dancing on leaves with your white spat-like eyes and new-fangled

steps. The scarlet and the black, cardinal red dabbed on with a paintbrush,

bodywork shiny as a prized *Cadillac*. Shall you be a welcome addition melting

the reserve of our stiff upper wings, joining us in take-off against a common

enemy, or a flying insect in the ointment of balance, taking over, a brash

importer of nylons and candy?

Day Seventy-Five: Bramble

White your flowers, with the palest nuance of pink, like a faded wild rose; thorny too, a distant, less celebrated cousin perhaps. The sister in the background, the less-cultivated, more interesting sibling.

You grow at hyperspeed, writhing through gaps, over and under, on and through. Upwardly mobile, stretching and grasping and not caring what you choke or scratch on the way to the heights, because you have no intention of coming down again. *Scarlett*-like behaviour and yet, such gentle blossom, blooms of delicacy, they will bring forth the richest, darkest multiple fruits in a couple of months. We will feast on them and stain our laughing lips with all the colour drained from your face.

Day Seventy-six: Raspberries

Like some of us you need a cane to help you stand, and wrap happily around our ordered lines, spiky but grateful. In return we receive punnets of tiny red thimbles made from berry clusters: bobbled hats, *Lego* fruit, holding together like rings of woolly stitches.

Tart and tangy, a summer sensation of sharpness that makes our shoulders rise and our eyes close even as we smilingly wolf you down on cheesecakes, in cordial meetings and greetings, tongue tied dates in pubs and fragile flirting on balconies. A taste full of memories of summer, intrigues and heartbreaks condensed into each deep red burst, none of which you let us take too seriously, mocking us with your London phantom silly sound effects.

Day Seventy-Seven: Geraniums

Pots of vibrant reds and salmon pink, fed on blood and meal, rushing to flourish and take the balcony by a storm of horticultural colour. Instant gardening in a cup and a choicelessly carnivorous plant. But still how you cheer, in your cheap abundance and hardy stock.

Favourite of those who use you like coloured sand in glass to spell out the names of seaside towns along promenades, as if you were squeezed out of a tube or rolled into Brighton rock. I wonder how you would deal with freedom, spread out in wild borders with room to roam, pot-less and unconfined, a rebel yell of chaotic growth, no-one counting your blooms or measuring your conformity. Geraniums uncaged, shouting, *"Geronimo!"*

Day Seventy-Eight: Ball

Lying in the long grass, sleeping in the rough, snuggling down into the cool, deep, green softness in hopes of staying lost. Away from shouting children and argumentative siblings, were you in or out? A four or a six? Best hunker down and leave them to figure it out for themselves, or wait until they run off bored of searching, looking instead for an ice lolly in the old *Bejam* chest freezer, leaning so far over they might just fall in.

Here you can slowly deflate, sigh yourself flat, let go and if you are found again, give out a disappointing thunk of weighty wateriness. End up floating in the pond maybe, a decorative patterned water lily, gradually discolouring in time, making friends with the frogs and the goldfish and the gliding, decoy duck that supposedly dissuades herons. Lie and look up at the sky and dream of other globes, more celestial than you, but less well-loved.

Day Seventy-Nine: Marrow

Mutant courgette, large and ripe, like a striped garden torpedo or an unexploded wartime bomb lying dormant in the cold frame, you sit, satisfied and sated in your fullness, enjoying the fecund roundness of your shape.

It seems strange such green and yellow, such dull flesh, staple ordinary tasting gourd which needs filling and stuffing before we can face it on a plate should come from your exotic lily-like zesty flowers, as though you lived all your youthful excitement through them and now lie middle-aged and frumpy, your waistline measured on *astro-turf*ed fold-up tables at village fairs, feted by and fated to the meridian of Middle England.

Day Eighty: Cherries

For the love of three – a conjoined stalk, symbol of a pawnbroker or of a fruit-filled triune. The ridiculous or the sublime. Deep blood red dripping sweetness and twirled absent-mindedly in our fingers, the holy dance of perichoresis and three becomes a blurred unity.

Birds on the branch, snails on the ground, people with punnets at the roadside, all here awaiting your juicy goodness and the tasty flesh of summer. Garden littered with stones that are hard and lifeless, yet contain trees; and your clever, succulent deliciousness that bids us all become your servants of scattering, like the women of *Eastwick*, casting the seed out beyond your reach, to begin again.

Day Eighty-One: Cocoon

Finally the waiting is over and you enter a larger world, a place of flying not crawling, a spacious place, free from the restrictions that have hedged you in for, oh, such a long time. A new body, a new height from which to see and understand the thing you are, the one you were, a viewpoint that encompasses all of your becoming and your role on the soil and in your prison and in the ether.

Left behind, like cast off grave clothes, like the bindings and shackles of hurting words, unravelled and broken, the cage without which you would never have known liberty. A transitional tube, a tunnel of metamorphic properties, an airlock between one plane and another. Mandela's cell, Lazarus' tomb, Mary's confinement: an enforced coma, a comma not a full stop, the place of waiting, stifling and stillness that forces us to adapt, to rest in hope, to believe. The cocoon breeds not only moths and butterflies, but faith.

Day Eighty-Two: Petunias

Gloriously heralding the heat of summer, the holiday season, oblivious to the horrors of hayfever, exams and wilting teachers sobbing over reports. Your bright and noisy colours trumpet sound, a brassy hallelujah chorus that breaks down the walls of our English reserve. We stand you on windowsills and house you in terracotta pots, knowing instinctively you will feel closer to your Patagonian roots in the sunshine.

Your plump pinks and deep velvet purples are the most decadent of garden ladies, your gramophone heads dancing a sultry samba in the softest of summer breezes.

Photograph by Victoria Dibbens, used with permission.

Day Eighty-Three: Leaf worm

As Blake sang from innocence and experience, there is no rose so perfect that it does not succumb, in the end, to the worm; no love without a measure of hatred, no world that does not engender a destroyer. All things must fall apart, break down, be consumed and remade.

Rot and canker, and sister death are as much a part of life as growth and laughter. Not causes for despair or desperation, but catalysts for change, birthing rage and frustration which themselves become liquefiers of suffering. What must arrive then? A letting go, a realisation that all is, in the end, transformation, and a knowing that something better this way comes.

Day Eighty-Four: Cinnabar Moth

Such beauty, the exotic *flamenco* red and velvet grey, opening up like a *senorita*'s fan every time you land, heart stopping colours flitting about the meadow edges of our garden. You clatter your castanets and stomp the blades of grass and the leaves of your poisonous ragwort nursery with staged, coquettish flourishes of petticoat.

I wonder if you are the escapee from the cocoon I rescued, and imagine idly that your dancing for so long before me is a gracious *gracias* before you fly to further fields. To God! *Adios*!

Day Eighty-Five: Honeysuckle

The smell of summer nights. You stir up memories of imaginary trysts on stone balconies, twisting your tendrils around trees and columns, winding your way into our hearts, your aroma drifting sweetly through the soft air like *billets-doux* between star-crossed amours.

Yellow, pale peach or white flowers, the fresh fragrance lures night insects to trumpets of nectar and wafts gently on the sultry breeze through the windows of dreaming poets and bards, muse to their dreamings, ghostly words already forming in their sleep, till yonder light breaks.

Day Eighty-Six: Campanula

Canterbury belles, swirling across the garden in your blue wild-silk crinolines, waltzing and whirling, moving gracefully with every breeze that gently shakes your *Mrs Anna* elegance.

Softest lilac in deep maroon boleros, you look like the blue fairy's hand-drawn wand or evening star, your five arms reaching out in love, wanting to enfold the world in beauty and perfection, to console the anxious *Pinocchio* in all of us, and make each one of us real.

Day Eighty-Seven: Strawberries

Garden hearts, round and red, wearing your seeds on your sleeves. Tempting and sweet, I'm told tennis fans eat you drizzled in cream whilst sipping champagne, but my idea of summer feasting is less fancy; counting ripe berries into bowls so we all get our fair share of lusciousness, picking you up by your pixie hats and dunking you in small heaps of sugar, grains clinging to you. So delicious in the cool of the June evening that the sore back and the sunburnt head and the getting tangled in netting seem prices worth paying now, as are all done things.

Day Eighty-Eight: Ceanothus

Bursting with purple cones of brightness, your Californian lilac flowers would

cheer the frostiest heart. Spreading colour wide and deep, royal clusters of tiny

blooms that bees and butterflies, as well as us, delight in.

Such a vivid blue, like a cloudless summer sky from your native land, watching

over *the Beach Boys* coasting the promenade in a *T-bird* as surfers run smiling

into clear, warm waters, where tans deepen and teeth whiten.

Day Eighty-Nine: Hosepipe

Coiled for so much of the year, hibernating in sheds or under eaves, covered in cobwebs or lurking in corners, coming out again for the short summer months when we charm you from your hiding places and do our rain dances around you, so you can't loop around our legs when we are not looking.

When your thirsty jaws are clamped tight around the tap and the water begins to flow, you start to life, jump and flex, snap to attention and flood with vigour, your sides swelling at your first drink after so long, the bulges glugging along your length like a python's dinner.

Irrigator, sprinkler, weather substitute, do you spend the winter panting like the deer, or like the first serpent in the first garden, do you bide your time, sure your opportunity to steal trust will open up soon enough, before you slither off to God's greenhouse?

Day Ninety: Ladybird larva

Nature's *Sticklebrick*, purple and orange mini-alligator, roaming the garden, zooming and consuming so much faster than your parents. Colourful and quick, I wonder why you need to stop for so long to change jackets. But flight must be your destiny and like us you are in a hurry to get to where you're going.

Purple must deepen to scarlet and orange dots become black spots. Your speedy streamlined omnibus needs to fill out to a round, mean, flying machine, and take on aphids, frying pans and fires. I shall name you *Clarence*, for we all want our wings, I guess.

Day Ninety-One: Mint

When I breathe in your freshness, I feel that newness is possible, that breezes of change may come, that hope is renewed. Such tender tips of lively greenness, your optimism rubs off even with the smallest touch, and life even smells different. Possibilities open up and the now tangible tangents of our future days seem to start closer to where we stand.

One aroma, one change of the fickle wind's direction, and everything could be different, could be better. Let it be so. Let your soft leaves be for the healing of the nation's hopes.

Day Ninety-Two: Swallows

Circling high overhead, deep upwards in the untamed, cloudless blue, you hold my spirits with you as you soar. A lifting and a rush I close my eyes to imagine, banking curved corners that smooth and fast, magic manoeuvring engineers can only dream of. And you dance around one another, diving in spirals, vertical vortices, like beautiful boomerangs hurtling in figures of eight.

Or perhaps we are flying above you, and you are rippling the surface of the lake waters, your sails skimming the wind and the flow taking you onwards and around, racing against as yet unseen Amazons and flying your pirate flag, searching for treasure buried still higher in the sultry air.

Day Ninety-Three: Gnats

Like the *"little foxes"* in Solomon's vineyard, you buzz around and make

yourselves a noisome nuisance, taking bites out of all and sundry. In the hazy

heat of summer evenings you are so busy partying your short lives away,

whirling gregariously in such a visible cloud, that you, voracious tiny vampires,

become feasts for others on the wing; dusk raiders, bats and swifts. Have a care,

lest you succumb to larger swooping opened mouths, scooped up like krill before

whales, or earth into diggers.

Day Ninety-Four: Sunrise

For those watchmen looking out with sleep-deprived, heavy lids, you are indeed their joy cometh in the morning. A new hope rising, a freshness of mercies given, a chance to start over, be ourselves, to let the light in, absorb the rays from the off, as the pinkly golden arms start to stretch and unfold themselves in their dawn yawning across the sky, pulling the sun up by holding onto the bedstead of the horizon.

For those of us caught sleeping, dozing, claiming lost hours of rest, attempting to stave off exhaustion or chronic pain, your light is kindly slow, softly glowing at first, and nudges the feathered chorus awake to herald your arrival. And if we miss this one, there will be another miracle of darkness chased beyond our lands in the morning.

Day Ninety-Five: Buddleia

Lilac lollies pointing out like spearheads, wafting your nectar aroma around the garden like irresistible insect incense. Pit stop for peacocks, tortoiseshells and admirals, your presence in the back garden of my youth was a lepidopterist's *Ladybird* book, a living encyclopaedia of butterflies.

Unfazed by our wide eyes, they drank with impossible tongues, lapping at length, unfurled and curled like silent party blowers, antennae outstretched, bulbous alien eyes and wings of such beauty that knowing no better than children, we would gasp. Middle-aged now but thanking God for you and the rediscovery of awe, of wonder, and of gratitude for such oases found in gardens.

Day Ninety-Six: Crab spider

Ghostly white, spectre spider, eight-legged translucent garden beastie, mistaken for a berry or a bud, yet a living skull and crossbones, web across the summer shoots, ready to welcome any myopic meandering meals into your sticky string.

Whitewashed bringer of death, yet cruel to name you solely for the fact that like all of us, you must eat. We hide our prey and camouflage our cruelty, your parcelled prisoners are in full view, clingfilmed for a late supper, and if we can overlook them, you are in your own albino way, a beauty: balletic balancer, sidestepping weaver, geometric genius, walking moonlight.

Day Ninety-Seven: Tomatoes

Gradually you grow in the glass house, inflating like tiny balloons, changing colour like traffic lights, becoming rounder and bigger like Miss Beaurigarde, till we can roll you away for squeezing, hopefully before your skin splits.

Fresh and vibrant, even your leaves smell strong and your taste is enough to match the most mature cheddar. Versatility is your middle name, brought up from the humble grow bag, you are good sliced, diced, fried, chopped, blitzed or ketchupped. Lycopene helps our hearts, big red and juicy like you, another of nature's helpful hints. Such goodness and packaging did not come to us by chance, but as a blessing from the vine, *pomme d'amour*.

Day Ninety-Eight: Mildew

Bain of the Israelites, and of apple farmers too. White powdery death that gives us curled, shrivelled, leprous leaves and stifles growth. Fake snow that will not melt, staining the tops of trees. Yet you are alive, and growing too, a fungal thread that also needs to make its way in a cruel world. Powdery being, perhaps we can think of you as downy decoration, or is your cursed nature irredeemable in a crop-based, apple-counting, fruit-obsessed economy?

Day Ninety-Nine: Dahlia

You grace the grounds with starbursts of colour, spiky sea anemones or petalled orbs, so many hues and sizes are possible, your octoploid status giving us untold variety with which to paint our herbaceous borders. Perennially beautiful and perfectly formed, the staple of the cottage garden, and yet your roots (well, tubers) reach all the way back to ancient American Aztecs, who used your bulbs as food.

I thought you were out of fashion, quotidian and ordinary, unremarkable aster blooms, seen everywhere, and yet so much lies beneath the surface. How little we know about each other in our feigned wisdom. Exotic creature, natural chromosomic wonder, well-travelled plant, highly honoured national flower of Mexico, now nodding your noble heads in suburbia, keeping your secret identity safe, incognito in England.

Day One Hundred: Clouds

We lie on our backs, the tartan blanket between us and the damp grass, our stomachs picnic-sated, and gaze up into the deep blue of home. Here we see the castles the Lord has built in the sky: the marshmallow menagerie of dragons and lions, of fairy faces and fantasies. Fluffy pillows, ice cream swirls, with trails of jet vapour cutting through our imagination like nails on a blackboard.

Shapes and shadows, grey and white, mackerel scales and flocks of sheep, sometimes tinged with pink and gold; the ever-changing landscape that, like suffering, passes us by. Weather leaving us altered and blessed by its stories and the clarity of His signature.

How wonderful that we can dive in, sail and soar, lost for a few precious moments in the brooding over and between the waters. In your perpetual motion, rain-in-waiting.

Day One Hundred and One: Woodlouse

Tiny pangolin explorer, garden lobster, car in the full armour of God that revs around the place, no obstacle too high, no miniature mountain too rugged. Dead wood or under carpets, nowhere is safe from your expeditions, as you sprint all over the ground on so many crustacean legs, as if you were a battalion of minuscule Roman shield bearers, holding your overlapping steel above your heads.

One second a tank, the next a hedgehog, rolling into a ball bearing at the touch of a finger. Beautiful silver defence, a master of efficiency, unchanged for aeons, and so familiar, we name you with affection: *chucky pig*, *granddad* and *cheeselog*, you wander our halls with impunity and our soil with speedy abandon.

Day One Hundred and Two: Cornflower

Who would have thought an alien eye on a stalk, an armoured pod in the green, could come forth from its shell like a slow, blinking tortoise, and be so decadently, confidently beautiful: a blue star, a firework exploding, a sharp yet gentle shape to enrapture any passer-by.

Perhaps we can learn a lesson from you in feeling freedom to become ourselves, to realise we too might be captivating inside, closeted in protective leaves that we can grow out of, ready to wow the world and discover our true and royal colours.

Day One Hundred and Three: Shed

Haven in the corner, at the side, out of the way. A place to retreat and go on retreat, maybe to India if it's a Grandpa Potts-ing shed. Tools and mowers live here, boxes of nails, hanging drills, hibernating hosepipes and secreted secateurs. Enough cobwebs to make Indy think twice, and a treasure trove of tat and boxes of buccaneers' booty waiting to be discovered by intrepid imaginations, both old and young. Mr Dahl wrote here in pencil at a green felt desk, scrunched into the corner like the balls of discarded paper around him.

The smell is dank and musty, the wind enters by cracks unseen, and yet it feels remote and safe here, amongst the maleness of things, the aroma of roll-ups and whatever got trodden into the soles of your wellingtons on your last adventure. No wonder the BFG and Fantastic Mr Fox were born here, no surprise the great glass elevator landed on this sacred ground, dropped by a child-like muse.

Day One Hundred and Four: Ivy

Speedy, shoots and tendrils seeking out new adventures like omniscient teens who cannon out of the door as the older, deeper stalks shake their weary green leaves and stick tight to the walls and fences they know so well.

Looking for the greener grass on the other side as we once did, hearts full of hope, and we stand and smile and know they will be back, digging into the dark, established places of home, and that it can't mean what it does to us until seen from far away, once mountains have been climbed and pigpens philosophised in.

Day One Hundred and Five: Fuchsia

Beautiful belles, dangling clangers, a flower to warm any campanologist's heart as you wave gently in the breeze, even if the tinkling is only in our imagination. Fairies may hear it perhaps, or newly decorated angels.

Such deep, vibrant colours can only come from God, dripping from his fingers fresh from painting the deepest parts of ocean and having tinged the sunset with pink. Luscious raspberry satin crinolines, with royal purple petticoats, you are the envy of every other bloom, none daring to stand next to you in fear of looking dowdy or dull. No need to hang your head, or droop with my exhaustion. Perhaps the boldness of your hues leaves you with no confidence of your own, or perhaps you know, like all the wise, that humility is the most gracious of virtues.

Day One Hundred and Six: Mouse

Daring darter, in and out of the burrow, the nest or the hedgerow you sprint; big bright brown eyes looking out for food and danger. They can come from anywhere, you could be surrounded by hunters as easily as we feel ourselves guarded by the love of Christ. Cats to the left of me, dogs to the right, crows above me, traps below me, owls before me, foxes behind.

Yet run you do, your tiny heart pounding a hundred to the dozen, nose and whiskers in overdrive. In and out, back and forth, to-and-fro, little brown pendulums hurrying time on, busy bodies, blackberry thieves, such darling cuteness, yet your family is a furry *smorgasbord* to so many.

How you must long for the day to come at last when the lamb can finally lie down in safety with the lion, and the mouse no longer fear the feline jaws, nor the lithe limbs that chase you until your batteries run out.

Photograph by Jeannie Kendall, used with permission

Day One Hundred and Seven: Bench

A welcome sight for weary wanderers and cramping calves; somewhere to fall sitting down and take the weight off. A mini-retreat, stopping off point, a quiet arrivals and departures lounge in the middle of the lawn, a place to ponder and take a new direction when setting off again.

Slatted seat, wooden pew, ready to steady you, to stand between you and gravity for a minute or two, base for philosophy whilst you toss crumbs to the pigeons and remember who you are. Arms to push yourself up from a prayerful time and return, a little more refreshed and contemplative than the you who sat down a few moments ago.

Day One Hundred and Eight: Crab Apple

A loner, you prefer one hundred years of solitude to the company of an orchard, standing tall and making sure everyone remembers where our daily apple has its roots. Yet despite your aloofness, you will sometimes play host to the druidic white berries of mistletoe and to symbiotic lichen. Perhaps you recognise in them, fellow hermits, oddballs, the plants and unquantifiable creatures that are beyond ancient, but which like you, possess the strangeness and authenticity of being one of a kind, the starting point of generations; the assembled aristocracy of the garden, the ones who have dug deep and determined not to change, strangers to adaption and despisers of interbreeding.

Blue-sapped and proud of it, your fruit requiring finest muslin to make it into anything edible. A messy, fussy process, which is just, as you see it, how it ought to be. Anyone who takes an apple straight from the tree and eats, deserves all they get.

Day One Hundred and Nine: Cabbage White

Scourge of the vegetable garden, where you lay your eggs on the underside of brassican leaves, knowing they will hatch into legions of munching devourers, doing Eric Carle proud.

Yet I don't think butter would melt in your mouth, only nectar, and small children everywhere thank you. Besides which, don't you flit and turn like the star of Swan Lake in your angelic white dress and reflect the sunlight, dazzling all with brightness whiter than anyone in the world could bleach you? Isn't your life a playing out of the transfiguration, lowly to lovely? No, I could never hold a grudge against such a heavenly being.

Day One Hundred and Ten: Pine Cone

Master of time and measurer of humidity, you scatter freely and wait for the exact and apposite moment to creak open, like a magic door, and send your seeds out into the wide world. The atmosphere is your *open sesame* and the treasure you release the beginnings of needle seedlings, who may grow to untold heights.

Nature's barometer, garden's grenade, you have pulled the pin now on an explosion of possibilities. Creation, planting, heaven's antonym to our sour, inventive destruction.

Day One Hundred and Eleven: Thistle

Scottish rose, Highland dreamer; soft purple that transforms into duckling's down next to thorns and bristles. Juxtaposed textures, the gentle and the gouging, the silk and the scratch. We can learn from you that beauty and pain, life and hurt are simply reflected halves, unable to be whole the one without the other, the two become one flesh.

Photograph by Cathy Urquhart, used with permission.

Day One Hundred and Twelve: Water Lily

Lotus flower, china teacup floating on your green saucer, how we envy your stillness. Absorbing the fullness of the sun or lazing in the shade, it is all the same to you, having learnt like Paul, the art of contentment in light or dark.

Drifting on quiet waters, dreaming through the summer, yet no mindless wanderer you, rooted in the deep, connected to the earth by a length of green, like a reversed diver's airline, you breathe in nutrients and are supplied and prospered by the anchoring in humility and soil that all the mystics know.

Photograph by Simon Roberts, used with permission.

Day One Hundred and Thirteen: Burrow

Garden shelter, deep dugout, mystery residence. Anyone home? Should we ring

or knock if *an ansr is reqird* I wonder? Voles, moles, mice or shrews, only night

time or the cat's jaws will tell. Life down in the mud, home in the humus, rooted

in the coolness of the earth. Do your paws shift soil blindly in the dark, your

whiskers feeling the way, nose twitching at the slightest change in the air? The

dark night of the soul where tangibility gives way to faith? But nocturnal

escapades are your habit, raids at dawn and dusk. Just like watchmen on the

tower, for you, the joy of sleep cometh in the morning.

Day One Hundred and Fourteen: Crazy paving

Mosaic of greys, your patterns are subtle slate. Final proof that size and shape do

not matter, as long as each piece can be laid down in willing submission for the

good of the whole. Just as each body part plays its role, so each shard of

brokenness is able to find a use and a home: to lose its sharpness in the act of

fitting, the balm of cement binding all wounds into a redeemed life, one

appositely making a pathway to new things. Surely this is the Road to Emmaus,

where all the loose ends come to make sense and lead to enlightenment.

Day One Hundred and Fifteen: Wasp

Master mason with mashed maché, you chew wood and pulp it to paper, mouth mortar and regurgitated brickwork. All of it becomes hidden castles and structures of Asimovian design, space cities, coned conglomerations.

You all look the same to us, yet each one of you wears a different mask of yellow and black, and your striped livery dresses a team, not a swarm. Fierce and strident, proud and fearsome, how I rue the boiling kettle and the poison spray and wish I'd let you live; even though you did sting me on my wedding day.

Day One Hundred and Sixteen: Pond

Calm reflections, cool stillness, mayflies and buzzing dragons brooding over the water, hovering in the heat of the day. Green algae and duckweed floating in abundance, masking your clarity, muddied mirror, darkened pool.

Refreshing difference, liquid light, here the skaters gently dance, and the frog heads bob and the goldfish dart, and the sun glances from side to side. Full of life, guardian to grub and grebe, leech and lily, slow of pace and reassuringly welcoming, parting for the dabbling of beaks and the trailing of fingers, and the dipping of daring toes.

Day One Hundred and Seventeen: Turnip

Round top of two halves, red and white, strawberries and cream. Swollen root, tasty tuber, ancient staple of soil and stew. How many people in the end did it take to wrest you from the ground in the children's story? Just like Rabbit and all his friends and relations in a chain to free Winnie-the-Pooh, you had the whole village turn out.

Large heart of the earth, your beet will keep us going for many meals. Mud-coated, you must be dusted off like an archaeological find, a vegetable amphora, garden treasure.

Day One Hundred and Eighteen: Slow worm

Misnamed *"fragile snake"* you are a long-lived, legless lizard, a roaming,

reclusive reptile. How smooth and secretive you are! Fleeting glimpses are all we

are likely to receive, that or your tail-end left shaking in our hands in fear as the

rest of you slopes off to regenerate, like an iridescent Dr Who, sometime

shedding your skin as you skim through the grass, becoming a new creation. The

original acid peeler, *Laboratoire Garnier* would pay a lot to know your genetic

secrets. I would stay in the undergrowth if I were you, rustling in the criss-cross

canopy of weeds, safe and silent.

Photograph by R.R.Wyatt, used with permission.

Day One Hundred and Nineteen: Blackberries

Early this year, after glorious sunshine and rainstorms, surprising us all with your bursting juicily upon the scene, hanging luscious from the hedges and taunting us dangling from the other side of the fence (where the berries are always riper).

Sharp and some a little sour, especially if you have "gone over" (gone over where?) but round with the fullness of bramble wine and sweet, staining darkness. Memories from childhood woodland expeditions recounted so well by Heaney, but summed up for me in the wonder of a rim-full ice-cream tub of fruity blue-black bobbly treasures to take home. Scratched, smiling and sated, even if, in our ardour, we picked more than we could eat, freeze, jam or crumble, it was the hunt, the gathering that was best.

Day One Hundred and Twenty: Gatekeeper

Holder of the keys, you are golden and bright saffron orange, spreading the

winged gospel of freedom everywhere you flutter by. I wonder if you take turns

with St Peter by the giant pearls above and whether you alight on the Book of

Life to rest from journeying to-and-fro between worlds. Certainly as we watch

you glide and take in your glory, it is easy to be transported through a doorway

of beauty to another dwelling place, and our hearts long to find their way with

you to colourful joy.

Photograph by R.R.Wyatt, used with permission.

Day One Hundred and Twenty-One: Greengages

Palest of plums, your fresh sage-like jacket confuses all but the seasoned jam-maker. I recall the novelty of green *confiture* spilling from a sandwich back when the orchard was steps from the house. Happy memories in your taste and in your difference. Maybe you long to be red, dark, showcasing your ripeness, or perhaps you relish your disguised goodness. Perhaps one doesn't need to shout one's fruitiness in loudness and ostentation, perhaps the proof of the plum pudding really is in the eating.

Day One Hundred and Twenty-Two: Bindweed

Curling like Jafar's twisted beard, wrapping yourself around anything headed

upwards, you hitch a ride, clinging to supports, hijacking beanpoles and ladders.

To make up for your misbehaviour, you give us white angelic trumpets, pure

gramophones that sing out clear beauty and like sirens, make us forget you are a

weed, a garden cuckoo, an interloper.

By such devices might we know all the wiles of winding wolves and slinking

serpents, if we had the wits to see.

Day One Hundred and Twenty-Three: Bluebottle

Shielded by iridescent armour you zoom about the garden at speeds and angles that make NASA engineers weep. The mathematics of your aerobatics is beyond us, yet your brain must be too tiny to see. With hundreds of staring eyes you sit, drawing your front legs across one another as though you were sharpening them, or auditioning for the part of a Bond villain.

All that ocular activity and yet your best sense is smelling out the steaming or the dead. Would you stay then, with Job on the dungheap, perhaps? Not judging, just knowing the way things are with an acceptance we find hard. Nature's binmen, a dirty job someone has to do, yet when we inevitably find you revolting, and swipe our newspapers and throw our slippers, all you can do is whine, *"You have deaded me again!"*

Day One Hundred and Twenty-Four: Fallen Leaf

Your green all dissipated and dissolved, you part company with freshness and sap, suddenly alone and falling. Down and down, lower you swoop, till the ground greets you. Different colours are yours now, burnished gold and reds, as though the sunset of your days has painted itself on your canvas. The light shines through your fragility and you glow like flame.

Everything falls apart in the end, and we all change from green to gold, fresh to old, full of life to full of wisdom. Breaking into your constituent parts, your molecules will mulch into the mud soon enough, not in grieving but sighing contentedly into the soil, a good end, gone on to becoming something more.

Day One Hundred and Twenty-Five: Rhododendron Leafhopper

I thought you were a tiny cricket, sitting there, waving your long back legs frantically, like a deranged semaphore expert. Were you trying to tell me something? A message from an alien world, perhaps? Or are you the Lassie of the insects? But then I saw there were two of you, and wondered if you were communicating your ardour or asking the location of the finest sap in all creation (and that you wanted it now). But my googling reveals your transatlantic nature, one invader feeding on another, and I do not mind. Such beautiful immigrants are welcome, even if your wild gesticulating is extremely un-English.

Day One Hundred and Twenty-Six: Hollyhock

Standing tall, like a series of periscopes ready to view the vista, you stretch

upwards and look to outgrow the garden wall. Bright pink or purple against the

sandstone, bees swaggering in and out of your trumpet blossoms laden with

heaving baskets of pollen. The summer in full swing with your colours

triumphant; flags of hope like vibrant bunting run up the green lines of your

long, strong stems.

Day One Hundred and Twenty-Seven: Sparrow Hawk

Today you fell from the sky into next door's garden like a dead thing, only to rise again with death itself in your talons. The hovering, the eagle-eye aim gone unnoticed. There was a flurry and a flapping, tiny panicked-sparrow squeaks, and then you were flying the scene of the crime. Long gone in seconds, a minute life leeching from your claws. A hole left in a happy clan. A drawn-out silence and shock. How fast the end can be, then.

I know somehow this necessary hunt is mourned in heaven, till we can all lay down in peace, and that every swoop of the sparrow is watched, yet I forgot for a moment that God and I were not the only ones with eyes to see and ears to hear.

Photograph by Kevin Thornhill, used with permission.

Day One Hundred and Twenty-Eight: Frog

Adventurous amphibian, springing across the path and into the undergrowth, a long distance from any watery home. We all make difficult journeys in life and find ourselves lost or stilled by fear at times. I hope you found your courage and your way.

Friendly face from my childhood that drew a delighted gasp if I saw your head, motionless as glistening rock, just above the surface of the pond. The only movement the random blink of an eyelid or the smooth, silent swallow of a brown throat. Strange choice for the makings of a plague, I always thought; webbed wonder, cool customer, leaping bounder that you are.

Day One Hundred and Twenty-Nine: Rosebay Willowherb

I remember learning your name from my lovely Aunt Ruth and rolling it around on my tongue as we all walked along the lane. Such a beautiful pink flower and so many delicious syllables to master. I was amazed to learn too that whilst you were allowed here in the hedgerows and sidings, your presence was less tolerated in the garden.

Isn't beauty, beauty? I wondered in my little girl's head. *Isn't life, life?* But there is cultivated beauty and beauty that has grown up wild. There is planted, deliberate life, and life that got lucky, seed blown in on the wind and settled in some happy place. Beauty that was meant to be and beauty by accident. But I say let all of it thrive together, blooms and weeds, wheat and tares. For how can we tell the one from the other at the end of days, except one grows in neat, orderly rows and one lets silken parachutes fly in glorious spontaneity?

Day One Hundred and Thirty: Wren

Small and dainty, the determined uprightness of your tail giving you away as you

hop along the back fence looking for dinner. Stripy arachnid-snacker, you rarely

venture far, no thermal swooping or high-gliding for you. Hedge nesting, cave

dwelling troglodyte, the quick darting of your long beak into creepy holes makes

you a regular Indiana Jones of the bird world; an intrepid archaeologist with your

brown jacket and hat. Unlikely hero, but then, no saviour ever looks quite how

we imagined, and large, courageous hearts sometimes beat in the tiniest of rib

cages.

Day One Hundred and Thirty-One: Feather

Have you arrived, like Hildegard, carried on the breath of God? Were you dropped like a heavenly question mark, gently floating down to-and-fro, back and forth to alight at my weary feet? Or thrown like a dart, to plummet into the ground, like a flag staking its claim on my time, a gliding gauntlet?

Your questions rest uneasy in my heart, wondering as it does whether I am brave enough to carry on being gentle, as your softness seems to prompt me to be. We all answer differently, some choosing the quill over the arrow, as Charlemagne might, the ploughshare over the sword; though some words are barbs and just as pointed and deadly. In the end it all comes back to the challenge given through Moses. Choose: Life or Death. Choose. Not as simple as it sounds, the curse of Hamlet, the questions raised by a feather, drifted from its home.

Day One Hundred and Thirty-Two: Crows

Black-cloaked harbingers of doom, bringing Victorian villainy to a garden near you, a murder mystery. You love nothing more than a good melodrama, an overkill, a feast of death. Up to no good altogether, when you nudge one another with hunched shoulders and mutter dark thoughts. Filling our heads with negativity, dementors draining hope.

You have another side to you too, desperately clever and chattering. Calling imitations, impressions, fast talking, quick thinking, using cars to crush walnuts at traffic lights and laughing so loudly it seems you might burst. Entertainers extraordinaires. Puffed up performers, always playing to the audience.

Bipolar birds, holding two extremes in perfect balance, something we have yet to master.

Day One Hundred and Thirty-three: Lilac

A true original, gifting us a whole colour, tall beauty that peers over fences and sneaks peeks over walls. Batons of mauve, gas flames of fragrance, a word that conjures up softness and subtlety, grace and sophistication, and whose syllables roll with a whole different emphasis Stateside.

For me, you are a teaching tree: the overriding memory lingers of discovering one cannot freely give others the answers, telling my teammate at age 6 that the other tree named after a colour besides orange was you.... And being told to stop cheating. Knowing you cost me housepoints and made my cheeks redden, and taught me the first of worldly injustices. But I'm glad I know you all the same. Ethereal lightness of shade, bounteous buddings, colony of colour.

Day One Hundred and Thirty-Four: Window Box

Potted planting, microcosmic horticulture, mini marvels; here the small things matter and the decisions are even more important to get right. Gardening by careful bonsai design from the calligraphy artist, maybe wild abandoned herbs from the chef, and cheerful marigolds from the one who needs to see golden joy more than anything; you could tell a lot about someone from the plants they choose above all others.

A sign of ingenuity, and of life flourishing despite all attempts to miss it out, you add a breathing space to the concrete and a death-defying, green holding on by its fingertips determination to the vertical uncaring of tower blocks.

Day One Hundred and Thirty-Five: Pipistrelle

Voracious insectivore, gnat destroyer, fly guzzler, friend to the clear air and the summer party, better than any repellent, you swoop and dive and grace the garden with aerobatic displays, navigating by sound and echo like aerial submarines, the twilight is your ocean, and you scoop up biting things like a whale engulfs krill.

Furry and cute, weighing less than a coin, Pippin the hobbit of bats, a Halfling mammal, delightfully dainty and softly squeaking, I know if I had a belfry I would want you to haunt it, hanging like clappers as you sleep, called out by Evensong ringing into the hunting skies of dusk.

Day One Hundred and Thirty-Six: Cinnabar Moth Caterpillars.

So now I see what all the flamenco dancing was about, as your mother misspent her youth flitting amongst the shallow grasses - she was laying eggs on the ragwort leaves, knowing it was the perfect nursery for her children: oozing zebra crossings; waspish wrigglers; looking like stripy sleeping bags as you chomp your way through the poisoned greenery, stripping it all down to the stems. No time to stop, even in the frying midday sun, like insatiable cormorants you keep on eating to feed the cycle of impending change, preparing to pupate under the surface of the world. And shall I see you come to cocooning too, so that the circle has come full round? I hope so. I love to watch things breaking out into freedom, imagining the same fate awaits me.

Day One Hundred and Thirty-Seven: Gardeners

Pottering parents, patient pruners, pea-pickers, they know the seasons and the sowings, the comings and goings, what likes shade and who wants sun, how to edge and dig and run twine up and down and round runner beans, sweetpeas and black eyed Susan's tall teepees.

They sense the frost in their fingertips and crack the frozen ground with hoes, fertilize and spray and water in the rows. Sit on deckchairs in the sun, deadhead roses when they're done. Secret ways are things they know, and all they do is done to grow, not just plants, but people too, and love and hope and marriage blooms right here in the garden with their care, a lifetime breathed in open air.

Day One Hundred and Thirty-Eight: Black Beetle

Like a black limousine you glide across the garden, your polished chassis glinting in the sunlight. When your wings lift up, *Delorean*-style, they take you swiftly onwards and manoeuvre you with a sci-fi elegance for us as yet unachievable. What hides under your sleek, liquorice covers? Are you a comic villain or a satin-clad sleight-of-leg magician? All I know is, you are a sure sign that black is beautiful, that dark is a delight; subtle sheen and dramatic night are married with style in your scarabic carriage.

Day One Hundred and Thirty-Nine: Hazelnut

Held in a holy hand, the universe within your subtly striped shell. Righteous reassurance, to know we are cosseted and cared for by a gaze so focussed, the loving look of the one who placed the tree inside your tiny form.

If we could learn to see you as treasure through Mother Julian's eyes, maybe we would bury you carefully too, like the squirrels do, and know you as sacrament, finding you a special place where sandals and egos are undone.

But as it is, the whole of creation falls unnoticed from the branches and lands with an unheard thud. So softly does the incarnation begin. Soon you will root yourself deep and reach for the sun, a new genesis and a perfect microcosm, life started over, the resurrection tree.

Day One Hundred and Forty: Bamboo

Mikado grass, sharp sticks pointing like a malevolent hairdo, a cruel coiffure, you menace and challenge like a game of skill. Were you dropped like this for us to take turns in picking your stems out? You take all dimensions by storm, reaching up and marked across, poking out sideways and who knows, maybe to-and-fro in time as well.

A clumsy metaphor for life perhaps, we foolish ones who dare to challenge the sky and stick our tongues out and sharply threaten, like snails shaking fists at the heavens. But we fail to see our own smallness, our slowness, and that our swords need to be beaten into better tools, before the real work can even begin, and that we are, for all our shouting and gesticulating, maybe just tapas for pandas.

Day One Hundred and Forty-One: Birdsong

Lilting lullabies and soft dusky tones, clear airs and delightful melodies that lift the heart, as if to say goodnight to the light and reassure all creation that it will return with the dawn, when you shall welcome it home again. There is no anxiety in your notes, no trills catching in avian throats as if they weren't quite sure of the message, hinting at doubts of sunrise.

No wonder the Lord, our twitcher Saviour, instructed us to watch birds and know their ways, and we should listen too, for the music that summons hope and wonder is here. Faith sings us to sleep from the hedgerows and joy will rise once more with the lark.

Day One Hundred and Forty-Two: Dragonfly

Zooming effortlessly
between the waters above
and the waters below,
God's messengers fly,
back and forth, heavenly
motor-copters, big-eyed
all seeing sticks. Denizens
of the dusk, friends to damsels in distress and display team extraordinaire. You
dart across my vision gaining *oohs* and *aahs* and then land for a few moments to
show off your lapis lazuli body-con dresses.

Metallic, iridescent loveliness, thrumming thoraxes of turquoise and emerald,
wings of intricate lace that rarely rest long enough for us to appreciate the
workmanship come from cosmic copper bobbins. That such beauty can reach us,
touch our hearts and set our vision ablaze is evidence enough of every good
thing. Joy and wonder and the fullness of gratitude, given in the garden.

Photograph by Jim Brown, used with permission.

Day One Hundred and Forty-Three: Jack-in-the-pulpit

At first protected by the safety of the green collar, the wooden surround, held aloft and aloof, away from the plebeian congregation of grassy blades and mossy mushrooms. Back then you dared to think yourself holier than us and preached away the early summer.

Encroaching garden by woodland, now comes the time to reap early words and you are either repentantly red as your youthful arrogance haunts you, blushing berries like cheeks aflame, or turned completely to thoughts of hellish brimstone, red passion a-fired.

Either way, you are bright scarlet now, your innocent whiteness all carried away along with your steps and your screen. Perhaps the modern church will change you, as anxious Anglicans time your sermons on their mobiles and Reverend Jill waits patiently inside you for a chance to speak.

Day One Hundred and Forty-Four: Dead Wood

A frontier city, Calamity Cockroach's hangout, hive of villainous millipedes to mill about and drink sarsaparilla with the best of them. A dingy den, killed by the pruning fork or the storm, knocked for six, hit by lightning, how long did you lay here wondering what was to become of you?

Death always brings forth life, and now you are full to bursting with creeping, crawling wonders. Larvae and bugs, ant nurseries and bee galleries and every kind of twisting tunnel known to insect kind. Life in all its fullness here, and none of it able to nest in your living branches; only after your own catastrophe could the murky myriad of workers make you its home. Proud and mighty tree in both halves of your life, perpendicular and horizontal, all is whole, all is true. Like Job's, joined together your history makes the perfect shape, perfect sense.

Day One Hundred and Forty-Five: Ragwort

Horses' bane, banned from Rohan and the pony's pasture, but bright and buttery in your cheerful, deadly blooms. One man's meat, you are food and shelter for the striped caterpillars and a nursery for moths. It's not for you to know who you help and who you hinder, but just to stand upright and zesty, being yourself and scattering your patches of sunshine throughout the meadow.

Perhaps you wonder why you are relegated to wilder corners and kept away from the choicest grass, thinking you do no harm and maybe, like gossiping meddlers, you would be shocked to the core to imagine yourself anything but golden innocence.

Day One Hundred and Forty-Six: Downpour

Rivulets run down the shed windows and along the washing line, drops of water rushing impatiently into one another and plummeting heavily onto the ground, joining their kin who come straight and mighty from cloud to earth, suffering no distractions on the way.

The surface of the birdbath is dented repeatedly by craters of liquid bombings, throwing crown shapes up into the air, meniscus shattered and no feathered friends to be seen, save one brave seagull determined to wait out the deluge sitting on a chimney pot. The path and patio pounded by pelting bullets and the sky thunderously dark. All heaven let loose, blessings pouring out thick and fast; I want to run out and stand, arms wide, open-handed, like we did once before, rain slamming into our skin and the laughter ringing out in joyful abandon.

Day One Hundred and Forty-Seven: Wishing Well

A pit where we throw our hopes and dreams, some carelessly, some with heart-a-pounding, some happy-go-lucky coin flippers, some earnest pray-ers, star talkers, hands clasped and eyes closed.

Tuppence taken for our thoughts, splashing over and dragging them down to your soggy depths. You hold our wishes in watery blessing, pondering them long after we have forgotten we came here. Always you answer with silence, or echoes of pocket change. Always you wish us well, and perhaps pass our whisperings, our inner longings onto someone who has a deeper claim on the desires of our hearts.

Day One Hundred and Forty-Eight: Seagull

Like a Georgian gentleman lifting his coattails by the fire, you arrange your wings and feathers before sitting on the chimney pot, settling down and closing weary eyes for a wee while. Eyes that see so far and work so hard, pinpointing pasties to steal and targets to pepper with poop.

Bane and blessing to the holidaymaker, you come to the gardens and the rooftops with great swooping and whooping, looking for handouts and leftovers and chasing off the smaller denizens of birdy surburbia. "*Mine, mine!*" you cry, claiming every crust and hogging the ground with your big flat feet, wings folded confidently behind your back as you strut down the crazy paving and take in what's on offer.

Lifting off again with cries and hollers that will always make me close my eyes and hear the waves crashing and smell the salty coastal air - of childhood holidays and now the Eastbourne ozone of my parents' cosy retirement abode.

Day One Hundred and Forty-Nine: Nemesia

Only half-hardy, staying indoors anxiously checking the sky until you can be tucked in your soil bed outside, no danger of Jack Frost nipping you in the bud. Your South African sap will rise to the summer sunshine even here and your many varieties of hue will lift up their lips to be kissed by the familiar rays of warmth, and sigh in contentment.

Pretty purple, gorgeous gold, ruby red, the rainbow runs in your genes and will let its spectrum spill out over the edges of tubs and planters everywhere, splashing like watercolours diffusing beyond sketched boundaries. My cup runneth over with splendour.

Day One Hundred and Fifty: Bird Dropping

Lucky for some, so they say, but like all mess, it descends seemingly from on

high and spreads all over the perfection we thought we had. The spoiling and the

staining of life, the after effects of feasting, the end result of process. But even

here there is treasure, nitrate nutrients, acidic wealth, gold in the guano.

Best then, to hold our painted canvas, our faultless lawn, our sparkling

windscreen, our prize-winning azaleas, lightly, so we are not fazed when

unforeseen passers-by add a dash of Pollock to our work. After all, splats

happen.

Day One Hundred and Fifty-One: Valerian

Soporific cerise, the vivacity of your colour does not betray your herbal use, and the deep raspberry bursts speak of energy and life, not drowsiness. Like the bright poppies that poison Dorothy's air, or the hurried droning of a nearly Sunday-lunch sermon, you disguise your sleep-inducing powers and lull us not only into a false sense of smelling security, but a soft slumber as well. When insomnia strikes, we shall tug on *Jupiter's Beard* and wait for his breath to fall gently down.

Day One Hundred and Fifty-Two: Barbecue

Sabbath suburbia where the last of the competitive men now fight their bulls, dancing round the primal fire in their uniform of "hilarious" PVC apron and baseball cap, tongs in one hand, fork in the other, drawn quickly from the cook's utility belt, macho one-upmanship is rife. How big is your *braai*? The range of your range?

Some women laugh, some sigh and watch their beloveds play with smoke, relieved to have only had to produce a cling-filmed salad. The *matador* men charge in, marinating meat, slinging their only 6 packs in the cooler. Proud Promethean Man pouring on the lighter fluid and joyfully watching the flames rise, admiring the sacred power, unaware of Elijah on the mountain next door, dousing his altar with the water of life and praying for rain.

Day One Hundred and Fifty-Three: Red Hot Poker

Determined to aim your fiery rockets at the sky, wanting to make a display of

oohs and *aahs* rather than the sounds of pain from solar-deprived dungeons.

Your colour rises like dawn, deeper at the tip where the sunburst gathers

vivacity, as though you were flushed through with fruit juices. I feel I could snap

off a bloom and savour it like an ice lolly, layered with cantaloupe, grapefruit,

orange and strawberry, zoom-full of flavour, zest-full of tropical life. Every ten

fingers fiery like Abba Joseph's, for why not become flame?

Day One Hundred and Fifty-Four: Pears

Hanging golden lime droplets, tree tears that might tremble and roll down its cheeks at any moment. Sunlit bells slowly twisting in the misty breeze, so that I fancy I hear faint ringing. *Williams' Bon Chretien* nestles near the wall in prayer whilst *Concorde* and *Conference* whisper cordially with *Beth* and the *Pitmarston Duchesse*.

You will taste delicious I'm sure: provided you are gently treated you will not bruise, and your tough resistance will become soft flesh for one special day that I will miss, no doubt, reaching for the fruit bowl either too early or too late. Only Goldilocks able to find the one that is just right.

Day One Hundred and Fifty-Five: Snow-in-Summer

Rampant roamer, spreading across the garden with your silver foliage, velvet leaves spiked like crampons as you climb rockeries and take over the bare patches, exploring everywhere keenly, redeeming the bad soil and claiming all aridness as your own private oases.

Starbursts cover the borders as your perfect constellations sing purity and give glory all across the ground. Irrepressible joy, bright whiteness of blizzard blooms causing us snow blindness, we gaze at you, happily rubbing our eyes.

Day One Hundred and Fifty-Six: Mole

Frantic diggers, tunnelling troglodytes, eternal excavators, you are becalmed only by the sound of the Javanese ear flute. Soft furry mudslingers, with paddled hands you row through the dirt, coming up for air like earth-bound whales leaving muddy blowholes. Your treasure is removal, the invisible, what is not there, the caverns full of emptiness and subtext which echo with what was not said.

Worms wriggle, but not fast enough, the blind eating the blind. Your subterranean subsistence is so alien to us, how would we see the world if we were a mole and we lived in a hole? Nature's hobbits, large-footed, velvet jerkin-wearing underhill-dwellers. Content to stay at home, not venturing far from your front door lest adventures overtake you, silent soil is your peace; though perhaps you might make room for a tale or two by the fire with Ratty, I can't see you messing about on rivers unless they flowed deep underground.

Day One Hundred and Fifty-Seven: Cricket

Green coat-tails folding neatly away and your ratchet violin with them, later you will bring it out with a flourish that makes me suspect you have Celtic roots, not least as musical magic and magical music usually comes from rain-soaked emerald places, but because you carry the fiddle and bow close to your heart and down your baggy-legged trousers. The sunlight brings on these cucaracha *ceilidhs* and the dating game too, with the same old songs playing long into the dark and sultry height of summer nights.

No sign of Pinocchio here, nor of strident advice whispered from our shoulders into our wooden ears, but only the insect dreams of one day playing a *real* sonata wished upon the stars that are so distant above both of us that size becomes unimportant.

Photograph by R.R.Wyatt, used with permission.

Day One Hundred and Fifty-Eight: Rusty Tussock Caterpillar

Cool name, conjuring Jamaican characters into my imagination with your pointy afro and your bright colourful spots. A reggae wriggler, body shimmering with poisoned tufts, and a tail that I swear you could wag, you leave me wondering which came first; tussocks, hassocks or cassocks, as you concertina your way around the picnic table, in circles, like Mr Rusty keeping an eye on his roundabout. Magic.

Photograph by R.R. Wyatt, used with permission.

Day One Hundred and Fifty-Nine: Garden Wall

Is your destiny to fall, with trumpets circling you, like Jericho's battlements, crumbled into your own foundations? Or to be rebuilt around Jerusalem, by a prophet whose heart broke for her exiles? Are you for keeping us out or keeping us in? Protection or Penitentiary? A stone boundary asks so many questions that it is always a place of wailing, of wondering, worth stopping to wait on God and ask for guided clarity. Am I crying or listening, waiting or building, coming or going?

Yet perhaps here around a garden, you are no fortress rampart, no siege starter, nor a limestone limitation, but simply a warder of winds, a shield, a suntrap, a guardian of green places and a keeper of stillness, with secret doors and creaking gates, old fountains kept safe within. A cloistering, caring, time capsule, holding the world and her rushing at bay.

Day One Hundred and Sixty: Large Rose Sawfly Larvae

There was I, imagining you were munching on rose leaves in order to become moths or butterflies, and find you are incognito, not caterpillars, but larvae, firefly-wannabees in waiting, cousin to wasp and bee, yet neither, imitator of fly but not one, master of disguise and illusion, your mother chain-sawed her way into the rose stem to give you a hidey-hole start.

Shadowy identity or missing insectoid link, you are nevertheless strangely fascinating acrobats, eating standing on your heads in spangled green stretchy leotards and chomping your way through your own bodyweight in minutes as if Mr Creosote ate chlorophyll. Maybe you don't care about classification, or being in the RHS Who's Who of garden pests, your mind full of the next mouthful, no winged dreams yet in your tiny head.

Day One Hundred and Sixty-One: Golden Rod

Bright butter flames shooting upwards, like yellow candyfloss a-chock with fake sunshine e-numbers, you bedazzle every passer-by with your blonde locks.

Blocks of *Solidago* savannah colour, you happily leave your meadows to grace gardens everywhere, visiting your aster relations and twinning yourselves with Nebraska and Kentucky across the pond. Ever cheery, golden gladness that will not tarnish, treasure worth storing up in our memories, tall tickle-stick joy growing on our doorsteps, heart-lifting close to home.

Day One Hundred and Sixty-Two: Ashes

Ashes to ashes, dust to dust, bonfire of the vanities left to peter out, die down, become a brittle break-downable concentrate that will crumble if you reach out and try to take it. The aftermath, morning after the night before, now the light and life have gone, acrid smoke still drifting, memories still landing their stomach punches, ignorance still grating this grate-full of faded embers.

A lamentation, hard rain falls on the powdery ground zero, and maybe the tears bring new life, joy cometh after the mourning, and inside the ash, the fresh, dark charcoal can be used to draw deep from artistic wells of life and help us start over, never forgetting, remembrance cut into our very souls, but slowly becoming part of us rather than the all-consuming, searing pain of the flames from yesterday, letting us make a mark and hold forever the line of a determined chin, the sparkle of a dark eye, a portrait of a firebird, rising, in sure and certain hope.

Day One Hundred and Sixty-Three: Bird box

Safe haven, nest with a roof and a front door, to-ings and fro-ings are less wild, but less windy too. Going up in the world now, from sticks and straw, no wolf will blow this house down and the Joneses and Jays have something to aspire to. But, a doubt breathes in your tiny beating heart. Are we building on sand or rock?

Shelter, refuge, but enclosed and dark. Progress comes costing fresh breezes in your feathers and the chicks will struggle to find another such place out of the cold. Are the old ways better? Would your parents think you had "settled" for depending on humans and deride your outings to lard balls and seed-feeders or would they be happy that you have an easier life? Perhaps such worries are best forgot, and the better chance you and yours have now worth gratitude. More time to shut your own eyes and dream of what might be.

Day One Hundred and Sixty-Four: Long Tailed Tits

Flitting in groups, stopping to stare and say hello, little Mandarin Emperor faces on heads that join neckless-ly to fluffy bodies, cute as tiny buttons. Hints of rust-orange eyeshadow, fallen dusted into feathers here and there, and arrowed tails like razor shells helping you balance on the washing line.

A troupe of teeny tumblers, amazing acrobats, so quick and nimble, one carefree unchoreographed display and you are off to a new arena, leaving your audience uplifted and applauding, hopeful of a return visit, however brief it might be.

Day One Hundred and Sixty-Five: Cyclamens

Tiny pink and mauve blooms bobbing in the lawn, delicate and dreamy, like a group of ladies gliding off to Ascot or a bevy of bishops with candyfloss mitres – precarious petal hats that look as though they might be carried off by the softest breeze, so much so that I almost expect you to reach up with green stems and hold them on as you laugh and joke; for how could a gathering be glum wearing the colours of sunset?

Day One Hundred and Sixty-Six: Wild Rose

Like a simple, one-layer petticoat instead of the full crinoline of your cultivated granddaughters, you sit elegantly here and there on your briar without concern for the fashions of today.

Your fragrance is barely noticeable, but there all the same, not perfume, but soft subtle scent. Your centre is not hemmed in and covered, so noses need to poke and bees bustle, but a shouting yellow egg-yolk middle waving the insects in. Generous pollen and nectar feast surrounded by white or hint-of-pink blush, you are the pure old stock who knows her wild, hedgerow origins and does not hanker for gold medals or fancy names, who sees simple is good and humble is home.

Photograph by R.R.Wyatt, used with permission.

Day One Hundred and Sixty-Seven: Earthworm

Humblest of humus eaters, so far down in the dirt that falling from grace does not worry you, you are content with your lowly state and know you would only bake dry if promoted to higher places. Aerating earth with your burrow and your untold miles of passages, your soil swallowing act. Your body a tunnelling tube, processing plant, munching mulch, self-contained within a wall of muscle you combine genders and even hold a bladder.

Night crawler, James is lucky to have you as his travelling companion, but Gollum uses you as an angleworm, or gobbles you up, as do the blackbirds and the robins, watching the gardener fork your world upside down at the same time as she calls you her friend. I prefer to think of you as a rainworm, dew-worm, coming out to dance when the thud of the downpour hammers on the roof of your life; writhing in the mud is your expression of joy, just as writing in the sand is mine.

Day One Hundred and Sixty-Eight: Rowan

Down by the pond, where signs say, *"Danger, Deep Water!"* you dig and drink till redness rises and fruits itself along your ancient branches. Perhaps your namesake will see you and emulate your ways. He who meanders along the edge of the river bank, but who cannot bring himself to the living water's edge to quench his thirst.

He who holds my heart, and pulls his roots up to himself, and no wonder, with the bad soil he has known. He who stands his own ground and has miraculously not yet been toppled by the storms, instead making his own circles of destruction as he swings his Viking axe and roars. He who is also *witchbane* and ash of the mountain, a fiery volcano of a proud and primeval race. May he see your rootedness, your red, russet robustness, flushed with life, and follow your heart suit, finally dropping anchor and roots here, where the water is healing sweet and the soil is full of abundant life.

Day One Hundred and Sixty-Nine: Goalposts

Some are the real deal and others just jumpers laid on the ground (isn't it, eh?), like all markings and boundaries, aims and targets, a temporary fixing in place, somewhere to fire at with our kicking, sometimes from the half-way washing line, and others from life's penalty spot. Fouls go unnoticed and unpunished, the whistle blows all too soon and the half-time oranges never quite taste as good as they used to, or how you thought they might. Did the ball go over the line? Was the scorer offside in the herb garden? Will we remember to take our muddy boots off before we go in the back door?

And the goalposts, which, contrary to public opinion, rarely move, simply sit or stand and watch, keeping score, hearing the questions, bouncing our best-headed thoughts back at us, netting shivering in the wind as it awaits the next pounding shock, and reflecting as a whole on our lives and always, in the end, throwing the ball back out and regurgitating all our impassioned direction.

Day One Hundred and Seventy: Storm

Rumblings and thunderings, grumpy god grumblings or clashes of Thor-throwings, rage-filled roars and pitchforks of pique, hurled into the earth, crashing into the water. Clouds pick up on the anger in the ions and jostle restlessly, getting darker and heavier with the atmospheric moisture that will end in tears before bedtime.

Is it science in action or poetry in motion? Both, of course, one seeking to explain, one to describe, this phenomenon that touches our deepest ire and wonder at the same time. Livid beauty, grey velvet rolling background to a dance of cracking sky. Only one hand can cast such violence forth and then calm it to a whisper. A divine *diminuendo* after the spectacle that got your attention and then drew you into a moment of awe, where the small, still voice can be heard.

Day One Hundred and Seventy-One: Zinnia

Multi-layered like a stadium of petals all crowding around the centre stage, such that I want to cup your trailing edges and lift them up so they can see. Rainbows sweep across you, each flower an artist's palette of every shade both imaginable and not.

Bright colours, happy hues, a beacon to butterflies and budding gardeners alike, we flock to your joyful displays and watch your painted plate heads on their many different heights of stalks, almost thinking they will start to spin. Or are they sunny *sombreros* from your native home? Wide parasols shading our British soil from a sun less fiery, powered by tea, not chillies.

Day One Hundred and Seventy-Two: Nuthatch

Sweet and small, sky blue cape and watery-sun yellow belly, with a long line of kohl across your dark eye that would grace Cleopatra's court. Tree sitta, wedger of food into holes in the trunk, bark-lifting vandal, beetling for grubs and wheedling for seeds, you eke out a living here and there, right way up and upside down, along and beneath, hopping and singing in short bursting lungfuls. Cheerful, well-dressed opportunist, abseiling avian, little lightweight bringer of colours from the waters above.

Day One Hundred and Seventy-Three: Spade

I want to call you a spade, but shovel is safer, though perhaps whatever you are will help me move the manure that is political correctness run a-muck like my liberties with spelling. A rose is still a rose after all by any other of its celebrity names. And you can still dig its root ball in or out of the soil, with the necessary muscles to help.

A large wellington drives down on your shoulder and forces you deep into sand or clay, the earthworms wriggling away and the robin sitting on the fence, head to one side, ready for a ready-meal. Strong arms rock your handle back and forth and all your labour is, in the end, about rhythm, removal and breakdown, digging the hard earth open like a cracking frost and putting in goodness or seed, taking away stones and weeds, changing the landscape, a benevolent blade, parochial ploughshare.

Day One Hundred and Seventy-Four: Autumn colours

The garden is enfolded now in a russet cloak, wrapped in orange, rust and gold, scarlet leaves and berries scattered across the once-lush greenery. Trees giving your focussed fruits to any foraging beaks, your warm mantle to any stranger passing, not thinking once of yourselves or the cold to come, with such generosity you will be hungry and bare come wintertime, starving and stark against the snow dunes. Yet giving is your glory, and the gifts come falling down from burning bushes; dancing sunset hues pirouetting in the wind and crunching underfoot; golden treasure raining down, yielded and lain before us like spreading palms, the only silver crossing them will be trails of snails, and though no holy donkey walks here, you know far better than we do, that every spot of ground is sacred and deserves your cascading carpet of colours.

Day One Hundred and Seventy-Five: Sweetpeas

Flowering sideways, too shy to open right up, too unsure of yourselves to bloom into vegetable pods, you nevertheless brighten up every corner of the garden where you are allowed to thrive, anywhere you are tended and spoken to with love.

Growing supported by twine or string, you are online companions, curling tendrils like phone wires and blossom like leant ears, always there to listen or give of your generous gentleness. Where would I be without your sweetness and your infectious wisdom, your joyous common-or-garden sense, your open-hearted giving? Certainly not here, my forum friends; not writing, not understood, not known, not accepted. My thanks inadequate, you have them anyway, for your soft, velvet love, my heart to fit your heart-shaped beauty.

Day One Hundred and Seventy-Six: Rosemary

Spikey mauls, you rise fiercely into the sky and fill the herb garden with strong aroma, giving little thought to your name, which sounds like you should be found knitting in a deck chair. No aging auntie, you, instead you are the dew of the sea, the Mediterranean no less, from sun-drenched shores and Latin lands, your ancestors fearlessly travelling and sending down their fibrous roots here in Britannia, settling for the island life and becoming ladies who lunch, Sunday roast companions. But as with most women holding needles, it is inadvisable to rile you, in case your dormant temperate temperament rises up like sap to your speared sprigs.

Day One Hundred and Seventy-Seven: Bucket

Catch-all container, you are always being filled or emptied, like a garden stomach, with weeds, flowers, compost, rainwater, or as now, standing under the overflow pipe, slowly filling like our stress reservoirs, the constant thudding splash that signals a dangerous level of angst, up and over, till soon you will let what is too much spill out.

In the mean time you keep the sun in your surface, the moon in your meniscus; alternate pail prisoners, fullness echoing light and holding hope in your drip-fed circle. Our cup brims over and the ripples run out to your rim in perfect roundness to remind us that chaos never wins.

Day One Hundred and Seventy-Eight: Blackcap

Welcome warbling winter sojourner and gnat guzzler, you wear the graduation cap that is awarded for survival, and your wife a copper mortar board, so perhaps you are different by degrees. Is she Sylvia? Your song wonders and wanders, up and down the scale, trilling with expertise.

I cannot imagine you making more serious courting pronouncements over the prisoner in the dock, birds being less prone to being judgmental than we are, though perhaps your tiny head might cock to one side between songs and decide on the worth and ripeness for eating of the bright berries on a particularly heavy laden branch.

Photograph by Jeannie Kendall, used with permission.

Day One Hundred and Seventy-Nine: Orange Ladybird

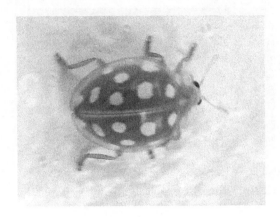

Like a 1970s lamp, a polkadot-patterned dome, you appeared, a light-seeking

orb, sitting precariously on my ceiling rose. You won't find any aphids there, so

I will climb up and take you out, wallflower, away from the wrong kind of bulbs,

and back to the garden, to leafy mulch and munchy leaves.

Seek a friendlier tree and make your home there, watching the seeds

helicoptering their way onwards, find a bed for the winter and glow in the dark,

like a little orange flame with white-hot specks, hauling in your legs to fold

yourself away till it is safe to come out and don't be enticed by electric suns or

fooled by fake fire again.

Day One Hundred and Eighty: Windfalls

Wasted on wasps, lying lost in the lawn, apples going brown and plums softening into mush on the ground, yet aren't you also a word for some unexpected treasure that comes our way? An apple falls, but by hitting an erudite head on the way down, some great truth may be made by a *Discovery*. A melting into earth may bring forth a new tree and fresh fruiting in time, a stone or pip carried far away dropped from birdish bowels into a wooded-scape, germinating into a feature that could stand in our green and pleasant land for a century, its damson descendants filling jampots for the WI into its dotage.

Falling is not the same as dying, and giving into gravity can be done with grace. Letting go is sometimes the bravest thing we do.

Day One Hundred and Eighty-One: Lupins

Like a meeting of Quakers, your blue bonnets rustle in the wind, and your congregations stand tall and proud waiting to be moved by the Lord. South American spikes, you have been growing up to the sun for millennia, feeding folk in Latino lands since ages past with your pre-Inca peas, your soaked seeds.

Bending as you climb, curving like a blade, pink or purple swords standing guard and keeping watch over nitrogen levels, enriching the soil and the view. Downy, silver-furred leaves, like rabbits' ears, compensate for your war-like, masculine shape, and like with roses and thorns, soft and sharp co-exist happily here as in all ancient things.

Day One Hundred and Eighty-Two: Fritillary

Misnamed "Flitillary", surely, and I wonder why ours are plain Green or Brown

and our transatlantic friends have a Great Spangled version to go with their

banner? We always understate our treasures, our Royal Mint is a little less flashy

than Fort Knox, and probably has a hole in the middle.

You are as fragile as you sound, and look like the deep dark orange-brown dust

on your midriff has rusted you stiffly in the rain, or will fly off you like faerie

dust as you beat your wings like carpets on your way from flower to flower.

Some of you now, so rare, you are almost a memory, like the coppices you clung

to for life. How shall we live without such balletic beauty, such gathered grace?

Day One Hundred and Eighty-Three: Yellowhammer

Your presence in the garden only a childhood memory now, so few of your habitats left in our urban sprawl, your begging song unheard except in the hedgerows, and who has "a little bit of bread and some cheese" to give you out there? I hope for friendly farmers and earnest ecologists, so you can flourish again and our borderlines be beautified once more with golden buntings.

Meanwhile may you hop and dive in and out of furrows, swoop and steal in and out of seed heads, and thrive in the edges of arable land, little darts of sunshine, butter flying.

Photograph by Kevin Thornhill, used with permission.

Day One Hundred and Eighty-Four: Teasel

Unafraid and tall, silhouetted against the light, with your spiky hat daring the world to tease you. Deadly serious, you march across the flowerbed like the Wicked Witch's soldiers. And yet, are you as sharp and humourless as you make out, I wonder? Each solitude standing is almost a cry for help, and your barbs a longing to be caught on someone's sleeve.

There is always the danger though, that you will be broken off and used in flower arrangements, or to raise the nap on cloth, or even, and how your noble soul must wither – given stick-on googly eyes for a craft fayre. But that is the trouble with those who pluck and cut and see your usefulness and beauty. To risk touch, to risk love, is to risk being left to gather dust in a vase with silken blooms, or to be given felt feet. But perhaps you prefer to stand proud here in the mud, forever going to seed.

Day One Hundred and Eighty-Five: Hydrangea

Had I known as a child, you had your roots in China, I might have found you more intriguing, but as it was, I mistrusted your green flowers that changed their minds and then their hue. Palest blue and barely pink, I held you weren't trying all that hard, ignorant as I was of soil having a silent *ph*.

Now I can see the beauty in timidity, the loveliness of pastel, the joy of subtlety, you are more appealing, and your clusters of tiny waxed paper flowers with their four wings seem like a garland of butterflies, all alighted as if by chance, in circular serendipity.

Day One Hundred and Eighty-Six: Pruning

Equinoxes seem to mean a change in the air, a deep intake of breath and a cutting back. A pruning of wayward branches, tempestuous twigs and rebellious ramblings. Things that haven't grown to plan must be taken back to the stub, nipped in their late budding and shown the right path.

Harsh hacking, laborious lopping and the bending of hooks, the tying of twine and the leaning of poles. These things will guide us, make us straight and lead us by the narrow way. Tough love, thy rod and staff, but not something understood until my life was made a *bonsai*, clipped and delineated, wired and boned, and now the blossom on the cherry tree shall have the *Samurai*'s self-discipline to settle for spring and the branches on the vine will wait for the leaves before pouring new wine. Nothing so patient as the one who was held back and learned to see the race with different eyes.

Day One Hundred and Eighty-Seven: Sandpit

A place for Roo and Tigger to lark and bounce about, a soft and sandy playpen, where Kanga can leave you and get five minutes' peace…maybe. A little golden haven in the garden where we can play lucky dip, no knowing what buckets, shells and treasures might be hidden out of sight, though we check if the cat is grinning first.

A rectangle of beach, where the ocean is our imagination, and the adventures in our heads are barely outnumbered by Abraham's grainy descendants. Pirates and buccaneers, maps with giant inky crosses, driftwood and contraband floating into our tales, turreted castles being built and defended here which time, not tide, will wash away. If only as grown-ups we could remember how to build stories in sand, and storeys on rock, instead of attempting it the other way around.

Day One Hundred and Eighty-Eight: Strimmer

Violent assault on the eardrums, industrial time-saving savaging swathes of garden that sees the cat darting in panicked starts over the fence and sends Small the beetle running, little lives leaving the lawn.

Single helicopter blade meeting ones made of green at speed and cutting every spear of grass down to size, showing no mercy. A level playing field now perhaps, but strewn with daisy diadems and cyclamen crowns, I wonder what price efficiency? Quick work means a short back and sides, no long-haired hippy meadows here. And yet, so soon, the green bounces, floral heads are raised, there is a creeping and a slinking return. The rebellion will be reborn in hope, as many times as needs be and always in defiance of the grass guillotine.

Day One Hundred and Eighty-Nine: Horse Chestnuts

Sticking out of the mud like unexploded mines, your green sea-urchins open to reveal glossy, chestnut-coated flanks; foals that will be measured not in hands but in the number of other conkers they conquer.

As we stood in the playground you could divine futures from tactics. The entrepreneur selling armfuls, the politician reeking of vinegar, the hero playing by the rules and letting the younger kids win, just occasionally. Now the nanny state has stolen the fun and the few spoiled it for the many, but back in the day the few who won our freedom perhaps began to learn of courage and tactics in these pitted dogfights, seeds on string trapezing through the air, blasting the enemy into bits.

Day One Hundred and Ninety: Victoria Plum

Glowing red and amber egg, a phoenix may hatch at any moment from your fiery

hues. Wasps and ants drool nearby, but the practised picker twists your stem and

takes you first. Succulent and full of the taste of late summer, with just a musty

hint of the autumn to come. Jams and crumbles beckon and the basket fills with

tasty treats, flaming fruit, oval sunsets fit for a queen.

Day One Hundred and Ninety-One: Guinea Pig

Cavernous cavy, deep gravy-brown eyes I could swim in. Your cuteness knows no limit and the way you gently hop around the run is heart-meltingly sweet. I could watch you and smilingly sweep your comb-over fringe, groom you and feed you nibbles all day.

The song of the Andes is in your heart, and I could see you in a mini poncho, tapping tiny tapered talons to the sound of breathy Bolivian panpipes. But your life and death in labs or kitchens I will not think of, for such things are unimaginable in God's garden, and only human beings could conjure up such nightmares. Here at least you are free to roam and munch, and live in grass and hutch, heart and giggles as you were clearly meant to do, furry, fluffy, fat Franciscan-friar friend.

Day One Hundred and Ninety-Two: Twine

Twisting stringy serpent, a cord of three strands not easily broken, supporting the weak and tying us to canes and branches to take the weight, keeping us in the vine, part of the plant, so we don't fall under the burden of burgeoning buds or berries, or lose our way in the dark cover of overhanging leaves.

Entwining edible edifices, running through the runners, stringing us along and taking the strain. You take no glory, want no medal, just the boring everyday box-string brown hero, there when needed, till then, like the rest of us, sat unravelling in the corner.

Day One Hundred and Ninety-Three: Groundsel

Grundy swallow, ground glutton, you creep into corners and are soon so tall and tufty that we frown and wonder how we didn't see you before.

Surreptitious masterly weed, with flowers that never really find the courage to come out and sit wrapped like tiny, common butterweed burritos on the end of slender stalks.

Everywhere you seed, come from flighty parachute drops, spies and secret agents, this bearded old-man-in-the-spring turning neat beds and borders into seeming scrub and wasteland, but at least in your untidy way you feed our flying friends, like a tramp on a park bench who miraculously finds the money for birdseed.

Photograph by R.R. Wyatt, used with permission.

Day One Hundred and Ninety-Four: Molehills

I seem to spend most days lately, laying on my belly in the damp, dewy grass, seeing things from down here amongst the mountain ranges that litter the lawn. It is all so hard and I'm hemmed in and hedged in by a maze of heights, an array of Andes, and a dizzying diaspora of difficulties.

I see sheer cliffs, high hills, Nepalese never-rests. But, when I climb to my weary feet, I can release the Tensing, and unclench my eyeballs, and see the world how it really is, just a few bumps that can be flattened, or left to bring texture to the turf, lumps in the loam. These garden behemoths are, from here, only bumptious bumps, and like a teenager leaving behind years of all-consuming acne, I can begin to glimpse a new perspective, where mountains really do move and seismic shifts of sight are possible.

Day One Hundred and Ninety-Five: Viola

If music be the food of love, play on, in your purple velvet doublet and green hose. Cross-dressing orchestral flower, stretching across gender and species, double meanings abound, *entendres* heard twice as strings and petals.

Small whiskered face of spring, now bringing your universal lilac to a winter garden too, following the sun across the sky, alpine tenacity in your sap, a bedding plant named moonlight, sorbet or jackanapes, made into a dainty perfume or a candied gourmet garnish, you are always a delicacy.

Day One Hundred and Ninety-Six: Cold Frame

Low down and dirty, close to the ground your Apache glass ear hears every

worm turning and the slow creak of cucumbers growing. Perhaps you have

aspirations to become a greenhouse, or perhaps you see yourself as less aloof,

more genuinely of the earth than such high-falutin' structures. Kew, Kew?

Barley there grew? I use compost, dibber and grub. No, your ways are humbler, a

toy town, dolls' house downsized, rough and ready, common as muck.

Day One Hundred and Ninety-Seven: Marigold

Ruffled layers, the petticoat petals in flaming colours *flamenco* across the edges of the flower bed. Fire in red, yellow and orange, dancing before us and making a solar system of small flaring suns to cheer and delight the heart's hearth.

Imeretian saffron, purveyor of fine spice and perfume, essential oil reduced from your rosettes of dragon's breath, or left to grow, each perfect round Mexican mandala resounding with the glory of its painter.

Day One Hundred and Ninety-Eight: Linnet

Rose chested songbird, pink as though tinted from holding a flower to your

breast. A tweeting triller and finder of the smallest seeds, such a delicate denizen

of heath and garden, drawn to flaxen foraging; freely forgiving, now you have

escaped from your gilded cages, you graciously visit us to give concerts and gain

converts and call out the Selfish Giant in all of us to springtime blossom that will

revive and renew our hearts.

Photograph by Kevin Thornhill, used with permission.

Day One Hundred and Ninety-Nine: Grasshopper

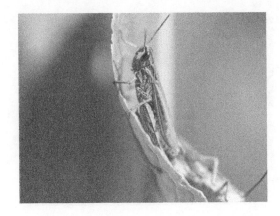

Orthoptera: your classification, big eyes and solemn face make me wonder if you run clinics in the lawn with your name and diploma proudly displayed on leafy doors. But perhaps your dramatic look is more thespian than therapist, your high-collared cloak hanging theatrically over your thorax, stood serenely sipping your *crème de menthe* cocktail, looking down upon those as short as Radar O'Reilly drinking their Grape Nehi (kneehigh) to you.

A *Ronseal* insect, that hops through grass and behaves as advertised, striding and stridulating in sawing song, legs grating teeth and ears in your posterior, you are the truly alien, welcome among us.

Day Two Hundred: Veronica

The true picture, Vera icon, imprinted on Berenice's veil, and the royal purple which behoves your holy history. Born of compassion, one kindly act brings you into our gardens, cultivated as shrubs from the smaller, daintier gypsy weed that speeds well along the sides of caravanning tracks and is spotted by birds' eyes dotting the ditch, the vale of Veronica.

There is no need to verify relics in nature, where every bud bears the image of its maker and shouts aloud the glory of his name, growing along the walk of his suffering, carrying us from Eden to Gethsemane, from garden to garden.

Day Two Hundred and One: Scarlet Pimpernel

Elusive, yet finding your way into all the cracks in the revolutionary concrete, your dainty flowers do not betray your strength and endurance. Bright red, like a poked out tongue at the regimented flower beds, and a poke in the eye to authority.

"They seek you here they seek you there, your clothes are loud but never square", a dedicated follower of paving stones, at home now in your English country garden, foppishly flopping fakery in Baroness Orczy's Kentish estate. *Zee big cheese* will never find you here, nor Trevor ever be surpassed, winding your way around the path of nobility and sneaking your way out of close shaves with the edging hoe and Madame Guillotine's blade.

Day Two Hundred and Two: Mimosa

Mistress of disguise, you sound so exotic, yet Hawaiian horticultured shades of you take to many climates. You feign sensitivity, curling your leaves at the slightest touch, but have chosen the sturdiness of Blackpool as your British home from home, where you and your cocktail namesake thrive.

Wattle, Acacia, and more Latin than is learnable, the names bloom like your flowers in fibre optic laser globes, pink, yellow, purple strands like Marvellous Mad Madam's Mimosa's hair, with ancient biplane fern fronds as verdant backing. Magical and wispy, soft and silken, delicate and determined.

Day Two Hundred and Three: Garlic

Van Helsing's veaponry, underground undoer of the undead, holy hand grenades hiding below delicate purple prettiness. Heart healing bulbs, your white core of self must be pulped, crushed and pulverised before it can become a balm and a giver of powerful fragrance. In such likeness and turn our red beating muscles must be shattered and ground into fragments before our aorta aroma can begin to make its way heavenwards.

In our brokenness may the Lord be close to us and bind us up, be it with a pongy poultice or ever-holding, unwearying, hallowed hands.

Day Two Hundred and Four: Pump

Time and a strong arm are needed to draw the water from below. Oh for the living water flowing instead from the fountain of St Teresa, or the *koilia* holy breast offered at Jacob's Well, all effortless and unceasing! Oh for an end to endless pails and painful shoulders and the ice cold chilblained hands of morning, or the sore heads of carrying. For an everlasting supply that needs no strenuous beginning, no fear of rust and seizing, like a heart failing after too little use.

But until that river flows, you are the hard-working, ingenious bringer of life, hydrating piston, rewarding effort in a way that at least we understand, drinking whilst we learn about free gifts and the quenching of other, more spiritual thirsts.

Day Two Hundred and Five: Greenfinch

Mistaken for a sparrow at first, on closer examination a flash of black and white striped petticoat as you preen and a green sheen on your coat as you turn to look this way. A dash of buttercup painted along your side and I see you must be a female finch, inching along the autumnal twigs of the crabapple tree, gorging yourself fit to burst on the overripe redness of its clustered berries.

And why not feast on the last of the harvest, the remnants of bright fruit, like the gleaners of biblical fields taking their share and storing it away against the harshness of winter? Beautiful Ruth, not as flashy as her Boaz with his butterfly display, but subtle, soft, gentle in colour and persuasively honest in her courtship, all tradition and kindness observed.

Day Two Hundred and Six: Chickens

The shed (the bantam cave) and your own Rhode Island run is out here and you strut and cluck and stop and turn, taking everything in and sussing everything out. All must be identified, food or danger, for a creature so low in the chain. I wonder you don't dislocate your precious necks, sticking them out and back and forth in a Max Wall Lambeth walk.

But here at least you are safe and sound, the nesting boxes full and warm, the seed plentifully scattered all around. And if some eggs are fostered by roistering roosters, there will be yellow fluffballs to gather and hide under your rusty maternal wings, like the children of Jerusalem. The fox and the cat may stand and stare behind the wire, but "fortunately, I say, fortunately I keep my feathers numbered for just such an occasion."

Day Two Hundred and Seven: Pergola

Framework for flowing flowers, cascading clematis, voluminous vines, a waterfall of wisteria. Clusters of climbing creepers, all making use of the opening of space, the ladder to sunlight, giving us a box of delights.

Lilaced lattice, a shady place to sit or to lead us through to another walkway, a protection from the harshness of heat, and the sizzling of summer sunshine, a planted parasol.

Day Two Hundred and Eight: Catalpa Speciosa

Rare and fragile, exotic creature, like something from the heavenly realms selflessly choosing mortality in order to beautify our lives for a short and sumptuous time.

Lily white and faultless, sacred female shape, every bloom of such porcelain perfection, angelic angles here for us to marvel at, hardly daring to look straight on in case, like most visions, you are best perceived humbly in our periphery and might disappear should we dare to lift our eyes.

Day Two Hundred and Nine: Water butt

Of a winter morning, grandfathers used to walk to the end of the garden and break the ice on you with their bony elbows, shaving like real men (back when blue furry creatures from Alpha Centauri were real blue furry creatures from Alpha Centauri – not this lot we have now). Breath heaving like fog and the capillaries shocked inside freezing skin.

I used to wonder at the greenness of the stagnant water in summer, when the edges were algae-ridden and the depths full of squirming wriggly larvae and things that fascinated and repelled me at the same time.

Rain hoarder, deluge depot, potbellied precipitation prison, here the wet is kept and the garden is watered from your tap, and who knows what tiny creatures cascade through the hosepipe after lurking so long in your cauldron cask.

Day Two Hundred and Ten: Siskin

A green finch but not a
greenfinch, small and lively
acrobatic doppelganger,
with your serious black cap
and go faster yellow stripes.
Barley bird, sociably trilling
and tweeting, moving in
groups to where the warmer weather and better food may be tracked down.

Raised in cages, like many songbirds, by those ignorant of your need to soar and
flock, unknowing of your superior claim to heaven's heights, the unfeeling
enclosure of wings that were always made for swoops and dives, epic migrations
and bird ballets choreographed by the call of the wild open skies. The caged bird
sings for sure, but how much more beautiful your freedom song, when thank
God Almighty the release of the captives is proclaimed.

Photograph by Kevin Thornhill, used with permission.

Day Two Hundred and Eleven: Sweet Chestnuts

Flat one side, round the other, like a dual world view, made to fit sweetly into your spiny jackets. Autumn bounty and smooth delight. You may not be horse-named but maned, a pleasure to stroke your rich, auburn skin.

Sat by the fire, you roast and make merry, an overture to winter songs and a prelude to harsh weather, the sumptuous nutty paste and the softness of peeled sensual flesh tasted on the hearthrug, outerwear thrown in a carefree pile of discarded casings, Jack Frost soon to be nipping at our exposed extremities.

Day Two Hundred and Twelve: Pumpkin

I have known people with minds like yours, all taken up with soft pie filling. But dug out they can become hard-headed empty skulls, whirling unfeeling atop the spindly suited Jack Skellington, King of the Pumpkin patch, thinking that everything has Hallowe'en meaning, when all in all it is a sleepy hollow, empty and cold, a time for smashing pumpkins on the ground before the gullible schoolmaster.

Perhaps, in the end, the softness of dessert is better, made for Thanksgiving and the carved out casing turned into Cinderella's coach. A better enchantment encased in pastry than ending as a glorified candle holder, or a grinning ghoulish gourd.

Day Two Hundred and Thirteen: Olive Tree

Were you gazing from your groves around Gethsemane's garden that sultry night? When the man-god entreated heaven, brow furrowed in foreknowing, and the drops of bloodied sweat falling on the soil? Did those heart-tears feed your roots and make you holier? Were you there in the wooden cross on that first day of saints, the promise of being taken to Paradise still hanging in the air in words too precious to fade, and the olive skin paled, impaled and broken?

Timeless trees, old orchard, now you remember him every harvest, as part of the offering that was lifted to those cracked lips is squeezed out of you, pressured by weights heavy to bear. The life blood flows out from your fruit, some of it destined to be anointing oil, used to minister and bring health, to consecrate and saturate, in the name of the one you watched over all those centuries ago.

Photograph by Dedo Mate-Kole Rampe, used with permission.

Day Two Hundred and Fourteen: Mist

Cloud covering the ground, sky descended, clumping in icy giant breaths across the garden. Laying low like a fugitive fog. Will you disperse gently, leaving a stratum of honeydew manna? Or just deposit damp droplets as you disappear?

Vanishing vapour, wisps of winter starting to enter the world, the heaviness of cold bursting onto the scene, touching the last vestiges of autumn unannounced and somewhat unwelcome after a lulling of milder golden days. A mantle of mist, a shrouding of mystery that will perhaps teach us about spiritual secrets and the patience we need to wait for clarity.

Day Two Hundred and Fifteen: Goldfish

The orange flashes zoom under the mirrored surface like a submariner's firework display. "Ooh!" We say, crossing the drawbridge and looking down. Such vibrancy seems uncalled for, extravagant, tipping the scales. But the heron and the gull do not complain, nor the creeping cat.

Comet fish, unable to help your bright neon beauty, you just radiate and swish, current in the current, electricity and water mixing, the only shock the surprise of such colour in the murky common or garden pond. Real gold, such treasure, is found in the most unlikely places, and once discovered, worth selling everything to buy.

Day Two Hundred and Sixteen: Bonfire

Time to check the dragged-in debris for cosy prickled sleeping bags, curled up

like Rip Van Winkle hoping to cheat the winter-tide. Now to place those

interlopers safely in hedgerows and bring the kindling: fragile foliage that cracks

underfoot, with fallen twigs, and lace them in-between the logs and branches.

Interwoven dryness, flammable lattice ready to go up like a shot, bursting into

burnished flame, skeletal leaves and rising heat, the whole shebang catching light

and becoming a blazing bonfire beacon, burning away this year's vanities, the

false gods and guys.

Day Two Hundred and Seventeen: Fireworks

Roman candles and golden fountains sending up smithy sparks and cascading ignited ingots. Sparklers spelling signatures slowly from small, mittened, paternally cautioned hands. The writing staying in the air, whilst the collective memory conjures up the smell of hotdogs with smoked onions, Blue Peter warnings and pets kept safe and warm inside but still shaking, licking their lips and hiding behind the sofa as if the Daleks were coming, tortoises obliviously comatose now in straw beds.

Catherines wheeling, rockets soaring, decibels so much louder than they used to be back in the old days. Everything bigger, bangy-er, more boisterous and anti-social. More expected now, no let-up in case attention wanders, the deficit unbearable and as Fawkes determined, the disorder palpably close. No understanding that the anticipation of the next one holds just as much magic as the gaps afterwards, that silence make a satisfying star sandwich, that the joy is held, like breath, in the waiting.

Day Two Hundred and Eighteen: Tree Trunk

Gnarled old skin, tanned and tannined, stained with years of weather pushing on the outside and the rings inside expanding and barely giving you a year to keep your girth in step, pressure from all sides, up and down, no wonder you crack. But the fissures stop the whole from disintegrating, and the gaps leave room to breathe, and that's what skin does, I suppose, like an extra lung covering the tree, pouring out and taking in, shielding and soothing, even my sore head today calmed by your aspirin healing magic.

So we hug you, and we carve our hearts into you, and deer rub you and grubs bury themselves in you and woodpeckers dig them out again. All life is here, in this one precious layer, the ancient atmosphere of an *arbre*. We orbit around you and thank the Lord for hide, for wrinkles and lines and armour plates that proclaim and protect life in all its fullness.

Day Two Hundred and Nineteen: Foxglove

Finger puppets in pink or mauve, freckled face on the inside, so that you always seem cheeky, like a little schoolboy out in the sun up to mild mischief. When small I imagined foxes creeping into the garden at night to steal you for mittens.

Heavenly horns, unblown except by the summer breeze, hanging pendulously like lilac udders, your milk, digitalis, made into poison to harm by Mrs Christie as well as the cardiologist's heart healing medicine. Are natural beauties always two-faced, or is it that we are too quick to find the poison and slow to seek the balm?

Day Two Hundred and Twenty: Winter Jasmine

A bursting forth in mildest almost-winter, an early entrance for which you could be hooked off the stage for untimely dancing into the fray. But still whenever you appear you are a most welcome wonder, an eastern princess pirouetting onto the platform, a glorious trumpeting fanfare of golden six-pointed stars that bedazzles as it bedecks the garden greenery.

Your delightful presence, a lit beacon, no creeping under bushels for you, no deft shyness, only buttered crowns and open unashamed beauty, come now, a nova in November like the Star of Bethlehem calling the wisest to follow your eager brightness.

Day Two Hundred and Twenty-One: Folly

Only the very rich can afford to show their eccentricity extravagantly in such playful folly, in helping Mediterranean countries lose their marbles. In the poor it is deemed madness or stealing, and entirely frowned upon.

But ostentations outside are amusing, and purposeless edifice one of the ironic identities of the upper class. Maybe now, like these loony legacies, their station is to be gawked and wondered at, the rest of us shaking our heads silently at the stupidity of it all, even as we shelter from the rain in the Bergholt Stuttley Johnson gazebo.

Day Two Hundred and Twenty-Two: Watering Can

Standing sentry, a tin soldier defending the garden from drought. You sprinkle life onto seedlings and encourage the growing denizens whether young or old, only aware of your role to give, give and give some more out of your watery wells.

Generous and gracious, you may not be aware that you have a heart beating under your riveted metal, but it is there all the same. No need to sing and dance your way to wordy wizards to know that this is your glad duty; you will hold rainfall and even brave flood and rust if needs must, and after you have done everything, to stand.

Day Two Hundred and Twenty-Three: Poppy

 You shouldn't be cooped up here in this suburban garden, but waving free as air in the fields, sistering the corn and brothering the wheat. And yet this too is a corner forever England, fought for and won, a shaded place where one might sit, with head bowed to the ground or with closed eyes gazing at the sky, remembering, never to forget.

Your silken petals are forever tainted, like Normandy beaches or Flanders fields, painted blood red and the image scorched into our minds, your freedom to be simply a flower left long behind. Yet the honour is worth the price, perhaps unlike our losses, and the deep poignancy of the poetry that closed the walls up with our English dead is felt still in echoes of harrowing words on war. No glorification here, none of Harry's *Harfleur* chutzpah, but only silence, the gentle breeze of respect, and the fragrance of history: dust; mud; fear; gun oil; the aroma of poppies, and the vague wondering whether anyone has yet learned the value of stopping the madness long enough to listen to the larks.

Day Two Hundred and Twenty-Four: Hibernation

Ready to doze along with darker days, the desire to sleep overtakes so many, finding cosy crevices and bedding down in warm mulch, on the underside of bark and the eaves of sheds, tucked away in the corners and snuggled down in nature's sleeping bags, wriggling till the casing is comfortable. The heart rates slowing and the pulses prolonged, the gradual coming to rest, like a series of dots ending in one full stop.

The trees too, snoring silently, and the sap stultifying, waiting for brighter days. How we wish we could join you! Yawning garden, sleeping soil, resting and renewing, hunkered down with the hedgehogs, brown leaves caught on our spikes, making a warm patchwork quilt, not thinking of blinking until the sun returns.

Day Two Hundred and Twenty-Five: Red Squirrel

Ginger nut-hoarder, keeper of the acorns and leader of the Tufty Club, with those spectacular wisped ears. Scotland has been your Highland haven and now you are come back in woodlands, there are gardens where you will be seen again at last, after decades of decline. Dear brother redhead, dear sister squirrel, you understand the sacrament of seasons and the grace contained in every small, found and treasured thing.

Such fine auburn fur, chestnut eyes, the bushy tail that could do a Rita Hayworth impersonation on its own, and the striking, standing pose that gives you a Noel Coward *hauteur*. Although it may just be a sign of forgetfulness, we look the same, stood still in the kitchen wondering what we came in for.

Photograph by Kevin Thornhill, used with permission.

Day Two Hundred and Twenty-Six: Tramp

The Lady loves you, and her son too: king of all vagrants. Their compassion touches you here in the dewy morning grass, covered in dragged-over newspapers, the words over your head and unheeded, what have they to do with your world?

Need to be going soon, before the homeowners interfere; cruelly or awkwardly. Up with the songbirds, you keep the best company, even if the company you kept, folded spectacularly, like the creased tabloids you carefully stow away for tonight. You rise stiffly, the cold shifting in your bones and the ever-present ache of hard ground taking its toll. Even a fox has an earth, but you frequent bank foyers and benches, forever being moved on, surplus to requirements and like your preaching predecessor, an unwelcome reminder of the poor, a thorn in the flesh to the lie of abundance and the hurrying-past-I'm-alright-Jack brigade. You smile wryly and remember being one of them. Part of you longs for a mattress, and part of you doesn't want to pay the soul-price.

Day Two Hundred and Twenty-Seven: Clematis (Freckles)

Droopy, hanging cream bells, golden clangers unseen by onlookers, unheard by listeners, this treasure only found by those with a nose for nectar. Bees buzzing all around lead me to look more closely, and like all those pointing their heads to the ground, your beauty is only appreciated by the world when your chin is lifted up, a finger gently raising you beyond shyness like a 1940s film heroine. Then we can gaze at your gorgeous, fuchsia-freckled face and be amazed. So many priceless wonders are thus hidden, their best facet turned down and kept for the few who take the trouble to seek. You remain undesirous of admiration, and focussed on the earth, the real, the things that matter.

Day Two Hundred and Twenty-Eight: Parsley

A cowardly lion perhaps, but your mane is rich, green and verdant. When you shake it in the wind, I can almost feel Aslan's soft warm breath, and I can certainly hear Dill panting loyally at your feet.

I know that you think the world wouldn't miss you that much if you were gone. A few fish sauces here and there would be without their *je ne sais quoi*. That certain something.. but not posh and ubiquitous, delicious and versatile like your Aunt Rosemary or Olde Father Thyme. Yet, I whisper to you in the kitchen garden, "When it comes to serving up cordon bleu, who do they place right on the top?" The gourmet garnish, the low lifted up to make everything lush and beautiful. A herb for the eye, perhaps, but no less lovely.

Day Two Hundred and Twenty-Nine: Mulberry bush

Here we go then, round and round, acting out the nursery rhyme and the age old killing, so cold blooded, so long ago. No crime scene, no DNA testing, no paper suits, you the only witness to the girding of the loins, the mustering of murderous thoughts, the dance before death, in the precincts of power, the cathedral gardens, where more than courage was summoned that dark day.

And now, all this is history, distant memory, so many long centuries ago. Your lot, all before you, the business of building purple berries for winter, and feeding up the silk worm, always so cruelly taken in a cauldron, cocoons stolen to clothe the rich. Do you feel anything about the immorality that surrounds you? Does it stir your leafy maroon abundance with a sense of injustice? Or is everything that happens outside and around beyond your jurisdiction, past your care? Out of sight and mind so quickly as we pretend as well? And yet, here we are, circling history again, thinking of Becket's ending, and the fickle hearts of kings.

Day Two Hundred and Thirty: Snapdragon

A reminder of when I was little and given seeds to grow, that instead of rejoicing in your velvet jaws, I looked sideways in jealousy at the tall lupins my brother had chosen. How easily we covet, turning from our own blessings and harbouring wants in our shallow hearts. I hope I have grown a little since, not tall and straight perhaps, but enough to know your beauty now, and have my heart sing at your knickerbocker blooms, your monster mouths that maybe really could breathe fire, though not when one is looking of course. Every child knows that, and sees your orchid-like, bizarrely shaped heads that convince them one could slip a tiny hand in and make you speak, puppet-like.

Lemon, burgundy, deep pink and orange, a fruity, *Zoom* lolly spectrum of hues, *antirrhinum*, nose-like, and a bouquet of memories, standing in the soil of time.

Day Two Hundred and Thirty-One: Wisteria

Wall waterfalls streaming down, bursting with lilac hue, taking everyone's

breath away and hiding wooded stems, twisted like cord, forming the framework

for flowers, happy to remain unremarkable the vast part of the year, giving their

chance of glory up for the one splendid month of adoration for the blooms that

flow and flourish. Perhaps if we all did the same and put our strength into

climbing and holding on, not wondering if anyone were looking at us, not paying

attention to impatient whisperings, but only steadying and readying for the one to

come whose shoelaces we are not fit to tie, focussing instead on the nesting birds

in our care, and the stability of our bedrock, maybe then the flowers would be

brighter, and cascades of colour would come.

Day Two Hundred and Thirty-Two: Frost

Crystallising cold, your icy patterns spreading across smooth surfaces, climbing stalks, reaching up to window panes and along paving stones, your fingers cracking as they stretch, the moisture hardening as the temperature drops at your heart-stopping presence.

Winter windscreens decorated in a delicate sheet, leaves layered, Jack feels his way, creeping everywhere, like a master of etching in every material, the silver scratches sparkling beautifully in the dulled morning light, cobwebs become gossamer glitter, the edges of snail-trails pinked and pointed. What an artist you are, for the garden looks like you danced in tiny blades across everything, like a skating sprite.

Day Two Hundred and Thirty-Three: Shrew

Your pencil proboscis makes me want to pick you up and write, but this nose is not for note-taking, and anyway you are too wriggly. Constantly on the go, eating lots and often, your whole life is driven by the need to feed, making you sometimes a little too daring and sometimes a little dinner for someone else.

Like Kate, you guard your borders fiercely except when the need to be kissed overtakes you, and then you will venture further abroad, though I doubt anyone will tame you, digger of dirt and forager of food, like a miniature mole, a velvet vole, master of the power nap centuries before we thought of it, or the bard took a fancy to your name.

Day Two Hundred and Thirty-Four: Swing

Between two trees, hanging forlornly like a sleepy hammock, you come alive only when you are used. A push-me pull-you motion, a garden pendulum, a place for a dainty shepherdess to sit and move genteelly, holding onto flowered ropes, or for a child to test their limits. Eyes closed, blood rushing, body soaring, higher and higher, arcing up and away, beyond the ordinariness of the world, till you feel your head is left behind and you must catch it up again on the backswing.

Stomach lurching, feet pressed into the air and all your might set to the back and forth of it. The ground beneath a sandy well scraped by braking feet, and the rushing motion has dug here too; a wind tunnel, a place for flying, where the mind is carried off in powerful imagination and all sober, grounded thoughts are let fly, as only fun can do.

Day Two Hundred and Thirty-Five: Summer house

Locked up now, bolted and tidy, time to wait again on celestial concerns, orbits and seasons, until your doors can once more be thrown open. There will be parties again, surreptitious sipping and clandestine catching of eyes. There will be trysts kept here with a good book, stockinged feet curled under deliciously, chores thrown to the summer breeze. There will be relaxation of rules, giggling and general larking about on the green grass outside, soft sighs, blatant promises and deep prayers all uttered under your roof.

But for now, there are stacked chairs, empty seats, the slow drip of an unnoticed leak, the musty smell of hibernation and a littering of dead insects on the sills. Now, even the spiders must wait and hope and muster patience. Everything has its time, and the long hot days will wend their way back, as sure as time and tide.

Day Two Hundred and Thirty-Six: Toys

Strewn about, *Little Tykes* have certainly been here, leaving their buggies unmanned and trainsets derailed and littering the lawn with drool-encrusted fabric books and cuddly bunnies. Evidence of fun and joy, birthday larks and shrieks, clapping and singing; colours, crayons and cake crumbs left on the grass alongside the memories and the faint echoes of play woven into the air.

And now in the quiet, mum and dad carefully lifting treasures and collecting favourites, toys lay smiling on the ground, happy aftermath, while inside the house, tiny ones tucked up, small breaths gently snoring, up and down, in and out, dreaming of a delicious dazzler of a day.

Day Two Hundred and Thirty-Seven: Rake

Now fan-shaped, when I was small, you were simply straight up and down and liked lurking in the lawn to trip up unsuspecting daydreamers like me. Lover of slapstick, in the space age you do the same chin-whacking to Ford, Arthur and Zaphod as you did to Buster, Ollie and Stan.

Then again, you used to be a bit of a card, a debonair charmer, whereas these days you are more of a helping hand, gathering up sweet smelling mowings, autumn leaves and mulchy mounds. Like so many things, gone from danger to health and safety, and your edges smoothed and curved. I wonder where the rawness went, and hanker for the days when my figure was more like yours and the only things out to get us were long handles in the grass.

Day Two Hundred and Thirty-Eight: Cloche

Stifling prison perhaps, but bell bringer-on of early bounty. The greenhouse effect in a small and false atmosphere. A tiny world, restricted and frosted, the plants inside see only through a glass, darkly, and we too, despite a planet-sized enclosure, are blind to the universe of possibilities beyond, the freedom, the space, the silence that might be ours if we could only look beyond our immediate confines, and wipe the carbon dioxide mist from our eyes.

Day Two Hundred and Thirty-Nine: Jackdaw

A true Goth, raven black and milky-lensed, silver sheen to your executioner's hood. A deep brooding darkness that carries intense intelligence like your crowing cousins. Nape cape of steel swung around you as you gather on lawns, in rookeries and linger near the newly nesting, waiting for a meal to make itself known. *Corvus monedula*, even your name sounds like a Victorian villain, melancholic melodrama, avian arch-enemy, yet you are a romantic at heart, staying true to one other, and you are not so cold-blooded, following summer, flying south for the winter.

Day Two Hundred and Forty: Toad

Dozing in the late autumn afternoon sun, sleepy and still on the step, taking in those last precious rays of warmth on warty hide before crawling off under a delicious duvet in the dirt for a long lie in. Eyes closed, you are easily picked up, saved from being picked off by cat or fox or mower. You are silken soft and light as ceramic, and I cannot resist the urge to kiss your lovely nobbly back, though thankfully this causes no transformation, unless it is in me, to see the beauty of a toad.

Here, then, under the leafy mulch by the fence, I will set you down. You cannot sunbathe in a corner of compost, but there is a better chance of your learning to caravan next spring, and if I hear a faint "poop, poop!" in the distance one April day, I shall put my head to one side and smile.

Day Two Hundred and Forty-One: Maze

Wandering around, dazed and a-mazed, one minute striding purposefully, the next face to face with a no-through road, dead-ended and hedged in, as Job would say, by God. Much like life then, this meandering, clearly planned but seemingly random pattern, which only makes sense seen from above. Still we keep on, like rats in a lab, turning this way and that until we learn to enjoy the journey, take pleasure in the constancy of green edges and the crunching of gravel and eventually find the centre.

As in spiritual searching, the middle is not about us, and when we find this deeper place we also find space, a place to rest and then freedom, and the way out to larger life beckons.

Day Two Hundred and Forty-Two: Cabbage

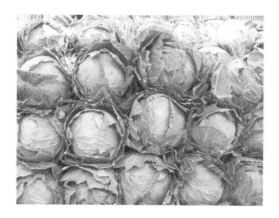

Your reputation precedes you, boring brassica, dull done-to-death school dinner, Charlie Bucket's soupy sustenance. But well-travelled information is never the whole story. You are lovely-leaved, big hearted, beautifully patterned, veins running through you like marble. A home for caterpillars, yes, but also a cure for mastitis and a soothing iron-filled side dish. So much more delicious raw or lightly simmered, or your redness, pickled. Not so tedious after all, your patch a place fairies and storks are drawn to, your softness somewhere to leave those who will grow into stories.

Day Two Hundred and Forty-Three: Holly

Prickly yet lush, deep dark green of winter verdancy and your paradox of life during the death of most leaves, the shining waxy smoothness against your thorny waved edges and the depth of opposing emerald against ruby berries. Christmas juxtaposition used by everyone from church to Coca-Cola in our season's greetings and our holly-day wreaths that shout out jolly grief in a mixed muddle of meanings and sloppy symbolism.

But still you brighten the world and speak of evergreen vibrancy in the short dark days of December, and the creatures that call you home, scuttling or nesting, are safer for your needle-like ramparts, and the ivy that curls and twines around your woody stems is your partner in more than just song, reigning together in the forest.

Day Two Hundred and Forty-Four: Washing Line

Hang it all out for everyone to see, the smalls and the mediums, the larges too.
Let them all blow about, bloomers and bras, socks and sweaters, woollens and
nylons. In the end the organic and the factory fabric, the designer dresses and
jumble sale jumpers all jostle together, pegged out and flapping, just like us, the
labels are lost and unimportant once you've been through the wringer. The
lifeline is one we all hold onto, and first and last don't matter here.

And when the rain or the frost comes and the wire is empty, little claws curl
around and let rest weary wings awhile, or raindrops slide along, colliding like
bumper cars until they all make one big sack of tears that gathers weight and
then falls, too heavy to carry, straight into heaven's bottle.

Day Two Hundred and Forty-Five: Rockery

Rocks of ages, pebbles from the beach, shingle and stones, and all the hard places in between. Tough plants, used to cold winds and hunkering down in crevices. Tufts of grassy leaves waving like horse manes and tiny flowers peeking above the fortress, making us feel comforted somehow, protected from the weathering that we must all go through.

When the colours come, we might imagine ourselves in Heidi's alpine meadow, goats bleating and jostling, Peter and Grandfather walking briskly whilst we dawdle with the heroine, gathering a rainbow of flowers, or perhaps when the white of Edelweiss blooms we find we expect the silken strains of Dame Julie's voice to echo around us, twirling like she does, enlivening the hills.

Day Two Hundred and Forty-Six: Runner Beans

Summer holly with your red blooms against a background of green. Slow, steady rising up the string ski-lift, all the way to the top with tendrils a-curling. Budding teepee with your maypole meeting point up in the sky, and you dancing around and around the twine.

Memories of shelling peas and drawing the peeler down your stringy sides, the pale purple pulses peeking from your innards and the cross sections dropping into the colander, like slicing curling Turkish slippers. Goodness straight from the garden, gorgeous, gravied greens, Sunday lunch, dug in by forks at both ends of your life.

Day Two Hundred and Forty-Seven: Slide

Three dimensional snakes and ladders, up and down, all that effort for a rushing sensation of speed, stomach left at the top and having to go back and queue up again to find it.

As a big sister or auntie, holding arms wide to make sure the little ones were enclosed, no danger of falling unseen, or we would wait behind the steps, voicing encouragement, like Timothy mouse piping on your shoulder. Then running round to the bottom of the chute, a human safety net as you shoot off the end.

I remember hot metal on cotton and red legs, and having to be brave when there was no-one to keep me clambering up with ever less steady feet, others pushing behind, and only tarmac or sand waiting to greet me after a clumsy, uncertain and squeaky descent. Standing up there on the top grate, staring at the diagonal lines in the metal step rather than looking down, maybe that was the first time I ever prayed.

Day Two Hundred and Forty-Eight: Stepping Stones

Look at the one before you, keep your feet on the rock and only move when you know it is the right time. Just like life, all timing and balance. Destiny may await on the other side but there is no knowing if the grass is lusher or any more green than the pastures we have already seen.

Rushing leads to splashing or the wrong sort of momentum, and worse still, the missing of minnows and ripples, unseen sparkling sunlight kissing the water and the echoing of memories just rising up like bubbles of soft sound from the shallows, left unheard. Take your time then, and enjoy the solidity beneath each footstep.

Day Two Hundred and Forty-Nine: Hyacinth

A Bouquet residence right by our feet, a bed of cultivated blooms, well-bred and behaved, with neat hairdos, no flower out of place, like perfectly petalled, carefully coiffured bluebells, mini Marge Simpsons in the borders.

How do you feel about the factory fields, cramped crowding bulb-producing lorry-loads and the juggernaut journey to the plastic pots outside the florists where few of you will make it to the airing cupboard and still fewer last until spring, to the magic of being planted out? I wonder if you would love to run rampant, grow wild, spill over from your shape, glory in freedom and rise higher to see the sun, non-conformist and irregular, rebels out of doors.

Day Two Hundred and Fifty: Late Bloomers

Just like you, my creative current got lost somewhere along the way. It didn't flower when it was meant to, or perhaps, just not at the same time as seemingly everyone else. Meandering, it stopped and did not ask for directions, got diverted, held up in the queue, swirling in the eddies of life.

But then, after tunnels of darkness, the longest wilderness winter, forty years of aimless wandering, there it was, handed back to me, brass-bold in a bunch of budding blooms: my flowering field; my musing meadow; like daisies in December, and Christmas rosebuds.

Day Two Hundred and Fifty-One: Swallowtail

Palest buttermilk yellow with powder blue skirts, you sweep majestically across the summer skies and are sure to be greeted with *oohs and aahs* wherever you alight, like a flying firework, a resting, arresting masterpiece of soft colours and dramatic kohl linings, size and shape borrowed from the tropics, two tiger tails protruding.

Sadly, you are no stranger to the pin or the glass cabinet. How twisted we are to want to capture beauty, not understanding that the lavender, or the sky, or the sunflower that backlight you, are part of the loveliness, and the breath in your tiny thorax, the hum and thrum of fragile gliding wings and the miniature heartbeat feeding friable veins all add to the sense of wonder. Dead and dusty, glazed and still, you are only a ghost of your former self.

Sunning in stunning serenity and the thrill of sudden seeing, far superior.

Day Two Hundred and Fifty-Two: Artichoke

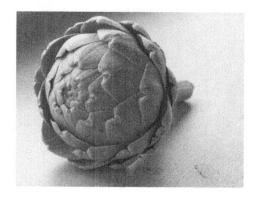

Giant thistle, supersized spearhead: caught in time, after budding and before flowering, your glaucous-green inflorescence has been food for us since Roman times, and in Africa, who knows how long before. Perhaps a prehistoric greengrocer had you in her display of delicacies aeons before you were introduced to Henry the Eighth's gardener by a travelling *Nederlander*. Who'd have thought a neo-vegetable that sounds like a wartime radio comedian would have so long and exotic a pedigree? But names are misleading and hiding in the quotidian can be the enigmatic and wonderful; a flower head containing an ancient healing heart; a pauper a prince; a manger a King-child, and the seemingly most ordinary of days, the centre of heaven.

Day Two Hundred and Fifty-Three: Carrot

Nibbled by famous bunny teeth, animatedly taking the wrong turning at Albuquerque and in asking the medic what's wrong. A tuber of vitamins, an orange juicing root, an underground storehouse of health, irresistible to naughty rabbits like Peter, especially when you grow in forbidden lands.

Allotment staple, garden familiar, your parsley-like fronds waving gently in the breeze all across the land. Bright soil light bulbs, impossible to ignore, in salads and casseroles, grated or chopped, so versatile and tasty that you lend your strong or subtle flavour carefully and seemingly without effort to any dish. *Julienne* or Irish stew, it's all the same to you, as it should be with us all, such classless ease.

Day Two Hundred and Fifty-Four: Statue

Standing at the end of pathways, as if waiting for us, placed where the eye will be caught and transfixed: religious icons; the victims of Medusa's stony gaze; the masterpieces of Moore, or cheap, mass-produced mouldings in concrete; gnomes and rabbits, half-clothed draping ladies, lobotomised fish with water dribbling from their gaping mouths.

Cold eyes peering out at us from within the overgrown undergrowth, fiction covered in ferny fronds and nefarious nettles, the mythological cast in stone, awaiting Aslan's breath perhaps, as we all are, in the end; cold and hard-hearted, wanting to feel that warm, sweet life-giving air, hear the soft rush of that still, small voice, to awaken to being and moving within his leonine Life.

Day Two Hundred and Fifty-Five: Twigs

Even Kings need to bow down to you if they are gathering winter fuel, for we are none of us self-sufficient and fires must be made in the cold, from the kindling kindly left on the ground by the trees, dropped and blown and given as charity to their human brothers and sisters.

Criss-crossed on the snow, like flotsam on a crystal tide. Or perhaps randomly fallen pick up sticks, for collecting, for making into a house for Eeyore, or playing games with; ready to be thrown head first over the bridge just to see which one comes out first, Pooh leaning over the first bar and Piglet under it, ears flapping, eagerly anticipating the Result.

Day Two Hundred and Fifty-Six: Tortoise

Broad-oar feet, wading through the grass, the lawn your gigantic undulating

paddock, through which you glide, pushing against the green waves and finding

your way slowly to the lettuce, the dandelions and other treats set out for your

daily picnic.

Reptilian skin, cracked and scaled, like crazy paving armour, and an inverted

kettle drum onesie that doubles as home and shield. Long, pink velvet tongue

that winds around the succulent stalk and betrays your soft insides. Carapaced

creature, what we could learn from your long-lived unhurried dreaming, if we

would stop and look into those deep, dark ancient eyes, set in moon craters,

mini-Great A'Tuin a-chewing in the garden and swimming through space.

Day Two Hundred and Fifty-Seven: Trampoline

Seemingly obligatory garden furniture now, we would have practically expired of excitement or at the very least, fallen off our Space Hoppers, to even see such a thing. Our shoes and socks would have been lined up neatly as we queued to have a go.

Ten minutes being Tigger and all that energy taken out and used up, bounced off into the stratosphere. Leaping and laughing, falling and knowing there is a springy place to catch you and fling you up again, just as winter has the safety net of another spring, after we have Fallen into it. And another kind of falling and another rebounding, reverberating renewal taught to us on Sundays. A different catching mitt, safe as houses used to be, bouncing back, like all things, from life to death, death to life, to-and-fro, up and down, oscillating between nature's laws and her laughter lines.

Day Two Hundred and Fifty-Eight: Grass snake

Just as at home in the pond as the grass, your moss green, mosaic skin snaking through the water, the slim arrow head finding frogs and finned gold delectably easy pickings, so that every time you appeared, we would fish out the keep net and you in it, off to the woods with you and a verbal warning not to return.

Silent and dark eyed, meandering like a pulled ribbon through the blades, winding and wary. How fascinating your alien ways and how beautiful the serpentine, mesmerising movement and no wonder the first of my kind could not help but hear yours in the smooth silence of her own innocence.

Day Two Hundred and Fifty-Nine: Potato

Humble, earth apple, our first American import and Raleigh's treasure, court-presented root booty, given to a virgin queen from a virgin land. Pocahontas' Peruvian peelers. How important you have become to us! Most versatile vegetable, turn-your-hand-to-anything tuber, salted staple, crispy chips and chipped crisps, baked, fried, sautéed, mashed, roasted, sliced and diced, with mayonnaise and chives in salad, hot, and gushing butter, topped with mint, or sizzling on a Sunday, setting us salivating.

And yet… so uninviting in the raw. Dull, hard, obtuse, related to Nightshade. Not an auspicious beginning. A lesson in letting things show us their value, to not dismissing the ugly or bumpy, the strange, the boring, the foreign. That brown lumpy mass, pulled up from the mud, sitting in the cupboard growing eyes, *that* will become deliciousness, given half a chance and half an hour.

Day Two Hundred and Sixty: Fungus

Skirting around dead wood, like captured saw blades held fast, or fairy spiral staircases, jutting out like Asimov's dwelling places, your amazing shapes food for active imaginations, our mind's eye feasting on your bulbous balloons, frilled petticoats and nobbly nodules.

Dusty death eaters, sending spores soaring, cloaking the world in Bogeymen, Fungus, Mildew and Mould. Repellent but fascinating parasitic gobblers. So close to the rotting and the damp, the dying and the crumbling, yet bringing life from the jaws of fusty death - aren't you the resurrection in the garden too? A roller away of tombstones, unafraid to venture in and transform all you find deep in the airless dank.

Day Two Hundred and Sixty-One: Honesty

I don't remember how you looked in the summer, despite your fragrant, bright purple blooms. I recall only your paper seed-heads, greaseproof monocles glaring at the cold.

Little frosted flags waving in round semaphore wondering why no-one waves back. Silvery-gold coins in metallic purses, and your name, so intriguing. Can a herb be honest? Can it lie? Is the truth in the eye of the beholder, perhaps?

I lie more to myself than anyone else these days. You can do it, you are going to be alright. I drag my body along, an unwilling conspirator in the web of fabrications. But honesty always wins and we must own the truth; enduring painful aftermath and exhaustion. What does a silent, shimmering thing know of such suffering? Maybe that is why your translucent cases fascinate us; their patent perspicacity holds us to account, their tremulous transparency feels more than we can bear to see. A living example of *examen*; allowing the Almighty to show us not only how to be seen *through*, but seen *into*. Visible vulnerable veracity, something unattainable, but utterly true, springing from the humble earth.

Day Two Hundred and Sixty-Two: Silver Birch

I never see your slender, silver, magical form without thinking of Narnian dryads. For it seems a sprite or sylph could walk forth from your delicate beauty with no effort, your trunk a door between worlds and a clear sign that heaven is nearer than we think.

Precious metal that we don't need to dig or pan for, just standing in the sun, available to rich and poor alike; dappled and papery in the daylight, mystical and ethereal if the full moon is shining. Smooth to the touch, and your soft sage leaves a gently cascading frame falling across your loveliness like a fairy fringe.

Day Two Hundred and Sixty-Three: Mistletoe

Builder of witches' brooms in tall trees, where owls may nest and screech, you attach your parasitic selves to sacred oaks, silver birches, holly too, and draw on their life, sap and sun to burst into clusters of olive green and pearl white, putting all your stolen energy into a winter display, like nature's snowballs caught in the branches.

Midwinter mistil twig, murdering arrow, Balder's doom, here you are now brought low, hung high to be kissed under, we merry Christmas Christians unaware of your ancient rites and scathing sometimes of those who still sup from a more ancient chalice. But all plants are brethren and all people too, pagan and pilgrim, each giving and taking something from one another, if we could only stop and see; look up into the symbiotic sisterhood you share with your host, seeing one not two, and a *Santa Lales* story and solstice journey to wholeness, instead of slinging our axes over our shoulders as we trudge out into the snowy grove to cut one another down.

Day Two Hundred and Sixty-Four: Hellebore

Our Christmas rose, grown from the seeded tears of a girl, come gift-less to the manger. But all things planted come to fruition in the end, even if all that grows up is a legend. Evergreen and ever-white, bright shining Bethlehem star, hardy in the cold shade of a wintry cottage garden or a breath-stealing night sky in December.

Your dark cousin used in medicine and poison, ancient ignorance claiming you to heal and harm, like your two-faced Janus name, made from stems of injury and food, you can kill or cure. Othello perhaps with his Desdemona, one driving the other insane, unwittingly, unstoppably, and the purest dark or deepest white are linked irrevocably in your poisonous family, your Borgia beauty luring us in to admire your angel petals in the harshest, barest winter days.

Day Two Hundred and Sixty-Five: Wendy House

Small house, a Darling residence, place for lost girls and wayward boys, hideout for fugitives, makeshift fort for cowboys, tearoom, spy headquarters and doctor's surgery. Anything can happen within these four walls, and probably will; landing on Saturn is not out of the question, and kidnapping Father Christmas may well be on the cards before bedtime.

How wide and deep, long and far-reaching is a child's God-given imagination! Here we make space for it and let it run, arms flung wide, the flip-top head opened up, the thoughts and possibilities whirling and leaping, forming the musicians, thinkers, scientists, poets and magic-weaving storytellers of the future; the ones who never ever stop playing and do not want to come in for tea.

Day Two Hundred and Sixty-Six: Partridge

Aha! What is this some cove-y has placed in my pear tree? For you are a walker not a flying fowl, thrown from the sacred Grecian hill by your uncle, distrusting, as Icarus should have been, of heights and drops, cliffs and falls, you feel safest on *terra firma* and keep your ear close to the ground, nesting low and seed-feeding.

But you have not escaped your jealous nemesis, for like your pheasant cousins, you will quiver and quail and grouse as the tiresome toffs come a-tallying and the beaters a-bludgeoning, desperately needing quarry as cumbersomely slow and uninhibited by intelligence as they are. With guns the odds are just about even.

Still, here you are, the first gift of many from the seeker of my heart, perched in your gilded cage made of fruited branches. By the time the garden is full of leaping lords I might be worried, but for now, Christmas is untarnished and my heart softly beating and untrampled. Maybe we will both escape the hunters, this year, you and I.

Day Two Hundred and Sixty-Seven: Robin

Your sacred heart emblazoned in scarlet feathers, a bib of tomato-soup brightness where the embers of the Christ-child's fire were brushed just in time from your chest. Caught light inside though, where the chambers of love beat loudly, bursting into song that lifts us higher than we know how to be. Beauty given breath from beauty, catching us up into the heavenly realms, a foretaste of flight and joyful worship we can only approach in wonder, sidling towards an understanding like an opera fan listening at the stage door or Moses peeking at God's glory from a cleft in the rock.

Photograph by Jeannie Kendall, used with permission.

Day Two Hundred and Sixty-Eight: Sprouts

Like Christmas visitors who've outstayed their welcome, we may have rejoiced

to see you yesterday, but on Boxing Day you are less of a delicacy, and

tomorrow you will be positively reviled. We will be happy enough not to lay

eyes or forks on you for another year altogether. But you are good for our

muscles, dear Brussels, with all that iron compacted into round green buds, or

miniature cabbages, and it is only overcooked that you fall apart, disintegrating

into tasteless school dinner mush.

You make me smile anyway, growing like Brassica baubles on your own little

Christmas trees, dangling-up decorations ready to be plucked, and for the sweet

story of Littl'un the mute meow-less cat who would sneak to the greengrocer's

shop and steal you away, mistaking you for small, green, blind mice to play with

or to lay as gifts at your bemused vegetarian master's feet.

Day Two Hundred and Sixty-Nine: Snow

Chaos on the roads, seething at the station; but here in the garden all is stillness, silenced by a cloak of crystalline crunch. A mantle of marvels, each small flake joined to its sisters. No two alike, no twins here, only miraculous microscopic individual icy wonders, tiny arms reaching out and linking like the touching of shining stars.

All made white and wonderful, every piece of dirt covered over, every dark corner sparkling, every stain removed, every eyesore eradicated. There is no place left untouched by God's magic, a flowing fleece, a softness fallen, a muting of mayhem that gives us the space and time to stop, to stare, to feel the freezing flakes brushing face and fingers on their way to oneness. A great joining on the ground will soon wash into watery unity and run onwards, like children rushing off to queue again for the ride, joyfully to return from the clouds once more, perhaps next year, perhaps this place, every time hoping to inspire awe and reflect heavenly glory.

Day Two Hundred and Seventy: Monkey Puzzle Tree

Not much of a challenge to a simian, since any child knows you are easy to climb, with your symmetrical branches and hairy hands held out, waiting for good things to drop into your palms of pine.

Come from Chile, now chilly here and yet able to thrive, reaching adulthood as we hit middle age, you might live for a millennium if high winds and axes will leave you be, letting you mature and spread, above and beneath, becoming all you were meant to be, a standing store of wisdom and edible seed, not a curiosity in an English garden, but an Andean oracle and sacred sculpture.

Day Two Hundred and Seventy-One: Detritus

Rubbish strewn across the grass, windblown flotsam and jetsam, come in on the blowing tide. Burger wrappers with their greased transparency, foil packets with remnants of crisp lurking inside, the ubiquitous cellophane, such trappings of fast food, labour saving and convenience that pile up more quickly than French fries, going large here in the lawn.

What do we leave behind, as we look back over a whole year and another Christmas made of feasting and indulgence? Is there more treasure than garbage? Or did we blaze a trail through the consumer superhighway, grabbing everything in sight in a sweep of supermarket salivation? Resolutions now being formed perhaps, to look over our shoulders a bit more often and leave less litter, remembering we are Wombles, keeping Britain Tidy and our gardens green.

Day Two Hundred and Seventy-Two: Windchime

Some find you a relaxing percussive noise, like metallic rainfall, that helps them drift off on the porch. Others, like me, hear you as noise, an intrusive clanging that gives the breeze a voice it does not need. But either way you are a collaboration, human plus nature, a sign that harmony can exist between us. A dingily dangling orchestral object, which somehow belongs here twixt the house and the garden, the made and unmade, holding the tension, guarding the meet of the whistling of fairy pipes and the breathing of those stood still, gazing on the threshold. Like the rocking of a wooden chair on the decking: a watching, a waiting for the bluster that might bring heavy clouds, weary and ready to wash the tired, thirsty earth.

Day Two Hundred and Seventy-Three: Doorway

Entrance to a secret garden perhaps, a heart-stopping, key-turning moment that makes our expectant hands tremble. So the doorway beckons to a New Year, an undiscovered country, a hidden cloister, an adventure in a snowy land beyond the back of the Ward Robe. Onwards we push, birthing ourselves into who knows what and where, out of bounds and into the unseen.

I will go on, but only if you will travel with me, holding holy hands, entering sacred space, sharing excited smiles of collaboration, we colluding cartographers of the New World beyond.

Day Two Hundred and Seventy-Four: Shadows

How long the darkness falls now from the past and the yet to come! Here at the gates of beginning, starting over, we feel the desire to let our monsters tear themselves away and walk slowly off into the night leaving us puffing our cheeks full of sighs, free to begin again, and yet soon, too soon, the pressure of needing to Get It Right This Time overtakes us.

The lengthening stretch of our potential obscures the gravel before us, as we take a new year's stroll around the garden path, but perhaps we might stop and remember that we can ask to be led. We can watch the light increase as the shadows grow shorter and the days longer, knowing that each morning new mercies form like dew, and not just once a year. For if our silhouettes were not constantly thrown before us, we would not have a following light, or we would find ourselves stripped of what is anyway declining, distraught like Peter Pan, forever chasing our own darkness and wanting to stitch it back on.

Day Two Hundred and Seventy-Five: Topiary

Not content with trailing branches, uneven shapes and fragmented silhouettes,

you craft growth into something other, unnatural, symmetrical or amusing. Like

giant bonsai battlements, leaves and twigs cut and forced, wired and swaddled,

footbound into a statement of your control. Here be dragons, peacocks, snails

and spheres, whatever I have a will to mould, creating with my secateurs,

shaping green and stifling growth. Or is it art, each hedge a blank canvas to

wreak your masterpieces on?

Biased, I prefer my buds and boughs natural, boundless, free to shape

themselves, but know too that wildness is unsavoury, too loose and unpredictable

for some, sitting on guard duty in deck chairs, reading about chaos theory,

getting up now and again to prune an errant shoot.

Day Two Hundred and Seventy-Six: Coal Tit

Bandit bird, with your black balaclava on tight, you bounce in the lower boughs

as they recover from your landing. Here you stake out the take out on the bird

table and check the contents of the flailing feeder as you huddle against the

freezing January wind.

Cheeky and chirpy characters that lift our chilled hearts, how could we watch

your tiny tumblings and feathered flouncings without smiling? Your wings may

be small but you still carry my mood higher as I consider the birds of the air,

laughing at such sweet *Zorros*.

Day Two Hundred and Seventy-Seven: Cobblestones

Like tiny stepping stones on land, a path that is hard to tread and a nightmare to wheel on. At first an unwelcome intrusion of the old city, of Victorian streets echoing with horseshoe clops into the English garden. But perhaps your different coloured pebbles might redeem themselves with beauty, looking like a seashore mosaic or a sand-toned display of petrified petals. In the freshness of rain you glisten like giant teardrops, and the lawn looks languid and lush in its soft flatness juxtaposed to the bumpy road that always forms part of life, and cannot go un-trod.

Day Two Hundred and Seventy-Eight: Fairy Lights

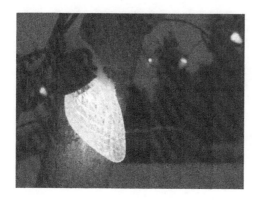

Alas my dears, Twelfth Night approaches, time to unstick you from reluctant branches and encase you in your attic attire along with tarnished angels, long-held-onto baubles and tatty yellow garters belonging to the Lord of Misrule. We will take care to wrap you snugly and like shampoo advertisement hair, detangled and shiny, so the next yuletide unfurling goes curse-free and more smoothly than this one.

Thank you for the cheer you brought, manmade in nature, yet strangely magical and fitting, like an unexpected lamppost in a snowy wood. Your bright lanterns each a fairy home, perhaps, with an illuminated incumbent glowing throughout the Christmas merriment, the whole line like a trailing rainbow cobweb thread.

Day Two Hundred and Seventy-Nine: Myrrh

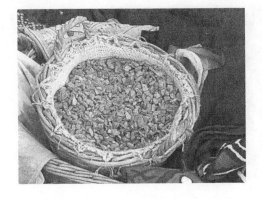

Your hosts may be grown in warmer climes than these, but we shall make a passing visit, just as those sages did in travelling far abroad searching after the star child of Bethlehem. For your gift was given out of wounding, from the repeated piercing of bark and the welling of sap, like nails pounded into another tree. The future echoes of bleeding and sacrifice came to the Lord that day wrapped as precious offering, warm and aromatic, like ochre, dried-blood red. For such flow becomes fragrant, a wounded healer, or the Balm of Gilead, one of many names he will carry, along with the hopes and sufferings of us all.

And does it startle others too, that the *commiphora* shrub that gives its life-sap to dry and darken into regal resin, is crowned in thorns? And will they repeat the sharp intake of breath I made, reading that its leaves are trifoliate, three-in-one, a perfect picture? If ever a gift were heaven scent, made with redemption in mind, it was you, deep, sensuous incense, hardened healing, prophetic, priceless present.

Day Two Hundred and Eighty: Blackthorn

Prunus spinosa, a philosophical bush with spiny thoughts as well as thorns, and crowns of white blossom, so you attract insects and repel intruders at the same time, holding out welcome garlands and blades *en guard* simultaneously, as perhaps we all warily do.

Come autumn your drupes droop ripely, fruit for foraging, to collect and jam in jars or add to the still, slow sloe for the gin-making. Mother's ruin begins in a respectable Victorian garden, tempting but too tart for tasting.

Day Two Hundred and Eighty-One: Stray

Bedraggled and wet, forlorn and unsure, a tiny duffle-less Paddington with no note, what shall we do with you? Let us offer shelter to the sojourner in our midst and find out where you truly belong. Let us give you space and not too much noise and fuss, lest you become anxious and flee, lost again into the unfamiliar, walking an unknown road. Let us find you good things to eat and drink, that you might be full and satisfied before we attempt your restoration.

Let us rejoice when you are reunited with family and watch with the sweet sorrow of mixing feelings as your ears perk up and your eyes brighten at the sound of another's voice calling a name which had not occurred, and let us allow ourselves room for the poignant pain of having done the right thing as we wave you off.

Day Two Hundred and Eighty-Two: Oak

Majestic, magnificent, magnanimous monarch-hider, king or queen of the forest, a tree for epochs, eyelessly seeing centuries come and go, stretching wide networks of roots and branches through earth and sky, only the grandest gardens can boast your presence.

How could everything you are have been contained in that tiny domed shell? Yet, like the universe in hermit's hazelnut, held in holy hand, it was all written there, just as my DNA clenches itself carefully around the spiral, guarding the secrets of my lifeline and my hairline, these palms the only ones worth reading.

Mighty and ancient of days, whispering timeless wisdom that travels on the wind, rustles in your leaves and burbles through your sap, here you stand, and still you stand, and we should sit at your feet and learn.

Day Two Hundred and Eighty-Three: Hedgehog

Prickly when defensive, the spiky wall-ball spiralled with all the softness inside, a hairy horse-chestnut, determined hibernator, hogger of hedges and hider extraordinaire. Yet when you do show your face, how sweet the wrinkled nose and lovely the limpid eyes, as you sniff along the ground, tracking sluggish prey.

Our vulnerability too is precious, our safe, open faces rare and fleeting, trust unmasking, disarming all. How we all protect ourselves so cleverly, with brutal barbs or tucking ourselves in and under, pinkest flesh out of sight, easy to wound hearts surrounded, fists curled around them, our methods just like yours.

Photograph by Jeannie Kendall, used with permission.

Day Two Hundred and Eighty-Four: Decking

Giving homes everywhere a naval extension, rife in the Nineties, was it *Ground Force* or *Titanic* that started the craze? Either way, whenever I look at your diagonal, creosoted surface I see Tommy with his nail-gun, grinning and rolling his eyes at the artificial deadline, or Mrs Molly Brown gliding gracefully, never so much as misplacing her parasol.

Modern verandah, perfect place for barbeques, evening drinks or rocking chair discussions on tomorrow's weather. Solid, artificial ground that will not give, your stilted air a little higher than I would like, longing as I am to see blades of grass push up through the cracks, a little green around the edges, just as I would be on any unsinkable boat.

Day Two Hundred and Eighty-Five: Dock weed

Having been stung, we search quickly for the spotty safety of your sorrel

harbour, a soothing, cooling sensation that brings *rumex* relief from the

harshness of nettles. If only every irritation in life had as quick a remedy, as

ready a balm, as easy an antidote. And yet, like an off licence and a pharmacy,

you often grow beside your nemesis.

Broad of leaf you are not only a convenient plaster for prickly heat, but

parcelling for pats of butter and packets of *lembas* bread. Nature's cellophane,

the original green packaging, proving we thought of nothing first.

Day Two Hundred and Eighty-Six: Privet

What Christopher Robin might paint on a sign if he wanted you to Keep Out, you hedge around the issue and protect people's privacy at the edges of gardens everywhere. A boundary bordering bush, neatly trimmed by those inmates, boxed in by box hedges, who stand on boxes, secateurs in hand, to look over, wanting to nose about, to see out but no-one to see in. So neighbours have always been, wanting a one-way, tinted glass stream of gossip, not "to be made sport of in their turn."

Evergreen, waxy leaves, like tiny Zulu shields, standing protectively in a line, always on guard, never dropping off on duty, alive and alert to any kind of rustling going on, tirelessly parading the outside edge of parochial England.

Day Two Hundred and Eighty-Seven: Gazebo

A wall-less room with a view, you make a resting place in the midst of greenery, a meeting of artifice and nature, the best of both worlds. A place to sit and savour every second, an octagonal oasis, a circular, cupola-ed calm, a domed moment's retreat in the midst of it all.

Breathing space, garden lung, refreshment by still waters or green pastures, no fretting under your fretwork, no coldness in your marble pillars, all is escape, inhaling sweet freedom, space to muse and be set upon by muses, to forge decisions or simply ponder grace, reluctant to move on.

Day Two Hundred and Eighty-Eight: Pot-Bellied Pig

Snuffling snout, investigating every snippet of straw, just in case. A little round food detective, on the trail, the Sherlock Holmes of husk-hunting; or perhaps, given your pigginess, the Clouseau of crunchy clues. Is there a famous Vietnamese Inspector? *Je ne sais pas.* But you glide gracefully around the pen on your soft, shapely trotters and know you are safe, precious piebald pet, held in high hog esteem. Unclean to some, maybe, but a roly-poly pudding of snorting scrumptiousness to others, and still to the swineherd son, a constant companion who does not look down on him, but loves him as an equal, in the lowly solidarity of all those so close to the ground, unlike us, who have forgotten our dusty beginnings.

Day Two Hundred and Eighty-Nine: Common Mallow

Mostly found along the edges, growing wild, you have sometimes been

persuaded further in, spotted in borders and coaxed into cottage gardens, tall and

purple, striped and beautiful, anything but common with your velvet trumpets

blaring, racing the delphiniums to the skies.

Your leaf juices a balm for stings and bites, and your cousins' roots used to

flavour the soft pink and white candy (which would smell as sweet by any other

name), all marshmallow pillow softness for laying dreamy heads upon. Maybe

that is why the sight of you brings Chitty Chitty Bang Bang to mind, a

connection between hedgerows, cottage gardens and children running wildly

through both the flowered green and *tout de suite* through the Scrumptious sweet

factory.

Day Two Hundred and Ninety: Virginia Creeper

Spider plant, spider plant, does whatever a spider plant does... well you do climb vertical walls using suction pads, so perhaps you qualify as a superhero, putting others in the shade and gaining admirers all over town with your beautiful red costumed leaves, your five-fingered hands holding on tight to the vine.

Walls seem ablaze with colour when you are at your finest, and the bright flames fade to a deep ember red as they get ready to fall, leaving a wintry trellis of bareness behind, preparing for a new batch of waxy green palms to appear in the spring. Each season brings a new outfit and a new "in" hue, a tide of tints that teach us to watch for the signs and know that change is always just around the cornerstone.

Day Two Hundred and Ninety-One: Rotavator

In a nickel nutshell you are everything wrong with the world. Noisy, dangerous and more powerful than you should be; annoying the neighbours on a bright, sunny day so the windows (and probably all doors) are closed to you; eating up petrol along with the soil and possibly Sophie's Dad's trousers at the same time.

Thundering along till the tilling is done; accident waiting to happen, maniac machinery, disturber of the peace, what can be done to silence your roaring?

Like all the power crazy, those who stir up the muck and don't care what impact they have, those who never look behind at the trail they leave, or the carbon footprints that chase them, you are arrogant in your belief that you are vital and endowed with the right to do as you please. Perhaps you could retire to Westminster where you belong and leave us in peace? Bring back the tools of quiet, the spade, hoe, rake and dibber. The soft, easy sound of sweating with the soil, not turning against it.

Day Two Hundred and Ninety-Two: Shells

 Brought here by
beachcombers, who,
brushing the sand from your
backs and knocking the
smell of the surf from your
inner spiral, the way Great
Uncle Vic used to tap the

ash from his pipe against a bench, now lay you down, empty and ornamental, in

builder's sand, part of a flower bed, pretty maids all in a row, or in a rockery

display with grasses waving like drowning kelp and twiggy leafless bushes

sticking up almost entirely unlike coral.

No seascape this, set amongst discarded snail casings and pebbles thieved from

the same shore as you. Shall it ever feel like home to a shiny, ocean dwelling

carapace? Or shall the sound the sea-shells sing in our ears seem like a soft sigh

for the shifting sands, a home-sick sibilance simulating the sea-shore see-saw

ebb and flow, the tidal suck and blow, the in and out breath rhythm of living

water; a depth of gravity you will only feel here when the moon silvers on your

smooth curled lips, pulling you back and forth like a lover's kiss.

Day Two Hundred and Ninety-Three: Yew

Guardian of gateways and graves, here you stand, dark and brooding temple

denizen, a paradoxical plant: all poison save the bright red olive casings, soft

abacus beads on green deadly lines, yet your bark extract synthesised to fight

cankers. Healing and harm in one place. Protector and poisoner, sacred and

sinister, so primeval and immoveable, yet lenient and malleable enough to bend

low in the wind and give yielding wood to make the very best bows.

Holding tensions and opposites lightly within you, all life and death here, no

wonder the ancients venerated your ways and called yew holy.

Day Two Hundred and Ninety-Four: Chimenea

Mexican chill beater, chilli heater, ceramic barbecue, keeping fire safely contained, lulling us into a false sense of security as we watch the flames flamenco gracefully on the logs or charcoal, flickering like our eyelids, ready to doze in the tempting warmth, so simple to forget your powers. Fire always needs watching, birther of planets and bringer of death, refiner of character and gold, Latin temperamental elemental, high-temperature – temporarily tamed, here to cook burgers and heat the suburban stone patio, and yet, in lieu of Meshach, Shadrach and Abednego, desperate to get your fiery fingers on that "Kiss the Chef" apron.

Day Two Hundred and Ninety-Five: Weeping Willow

Down by the water's edge, by the Rivers of Babylon, you sat down and wept, and never left. Here the tears come in torrents, unstoppable droplets linked in leafy chains of cascading green, like the soft hair of a maiden tree. Will you one day shake your lion's mane and roar out in pain, or always softly, softly, head bowed, keep the waterfalls flowing?

Sorrow has no fences, grief no limits. This is your space for letting it all out with no thought of whether a passing prince might one day climb up the tumbling tresses and plant a kiss on your trunk to halt your hopelessness (though he might).

Let despair have its day and be beautiful in your brokenness. All your teardrops are collected in rivers of living water within the bottles of the King. Weep then, in his courtyards and do not be ashamed. Lamentations release royal healing and are needed perhaps now more than ever.

Day Two Hundred and Ninety-Six: Little Owl

Small Athenian carrier of wisdom, calling in the streets and gardens, proverbial purveyor of knowledge and mystery, hunting in the half-light, winging in the dawn and dusk, crepuscular creature, coming alive at the edges of time.

Tiny, rounded, feathered ball of bobbing bumptiousness, eyes like headlights, yellow and bigger than your belly, a swooping display of spherical aeronautics, what would our flights look like if they had been modelled on you? Dear "wol", with your talonned grasp of language, and your conceited, cobbled calligraphy. For who needs to know more than how to spell Tuesday, even if all the letters are "not necessarily in the right order?"

Day Two Hundred and Ninety-Seven: Pampas Grass

Billowing in the British breeze, standing alone in your gigantic island clump surrounded by an emerald isle of lawn, I wonder how you got here from those South American plains, where you grow in swaying swathes, meandering in Amazon country and not conspicuous and incongruous as here, next to beds of primulas and rows of roses. Did you arrive, Paddington-like, on the same boat perhaps, with a note around your roots, shivering in the northern cold?

No duffle coat for you, but adopted by seventies' suburbia and planted out so near bricks and mortar as to make you feel hemmed in, and not a *gaucho* in sight, nor the sultry savannah winds to warm you, but only cold, such cold in your very blades, that vicious chill that will even make you glad to let your luscious plumes sit, musty and dead in vases with silk orchids on shelves and atop cabinets, fussed by doppelganger feather dusters, *anything* so long as it is indoors.

Day Two Hundred and Ninety-Eight: Scots Pine

Highland flinging your Caledonian cones beyond your canopy, you stand tall and proud on the Scottish slopes, ancient wood that has seen off all invaders (not to mention an ice age) and lived to tell the tale. Now widespread in a diaspora across continents, and yes, snuck into corners of gardens, still only here in your homeland are you clustered together as the only purebred Gregor clan conifer.

On Burns' Night, you rustle your evergreen boughs wherever you are rooted, and recite Rabbie's rhymes in proud readings, relishing rolling those rrrrs for a red, red rose. Tree of Scotland, branches beating in the dark, bonnie bairns everywhere tucked into beds with bard's fond kiss, as the piped in puddin-race begins.

Day Two Hundred and Ninety-Nine: Eucalyptus

Keeper of koala cuddles, you are never one to follow the flock, casting convention to the wind and swapping petals for stamens, making flowers that look like pink or white hula skirts swaying in the breeze, just right for your tropical provenance, or perhaps they are little octopi waving tassel-like tentacles in the tides, or upside-down down under curtain tie bell-pulls.

A teenage hippy, oil glands run amok and rainbows running through your bark, a peace-loving, non-violent sitter-in in the garden, whether bush or tree, mallee, mallet or marlock, magic marsupial-minding myrtle marvels.

Day Three Hundred: Fountain

Spiritual consolations flow easily here from the Source of life itself, from the *koilia* of Christ, living water pouring into the basin of our hearts so that we may never thirst again. All need held out in prayer is effortlessly quenched by such an outpouring; we cup and dip our hands till they run over, drinking the divine down, refreshed by this royal rivulet streaming from the sanctuary.

Ezekiel's angel may measure the distance in cubits, but our new Samaritan friend will need to haul no more pails, and Teresa tells us we may stand by this cascade of sweetness which will deliver delight to every part of us as a gift from God himself.

Day Three Hundred and One: Mahonia

Flowered fingers reaching out, a splayed sunburst of soft yellow against racing green in the winter sun. Tiny golden cowbells dangling down, bringing with their imagined tinkling, thoughts of Alpine meadows. An unexpected, joyous song in these frozen days when sound carries further. An arresting aroma startling a stray walker or a gardener come to graft, to prepare hard ground, not expecting such treasure to be trumpeted, heralding glory so early in the year. We breathe you in and gaze transfixed by the memory of summer colour, like commuters trapped in headlights.

Day Three Hundred and Two: Fairies

Blithe spirited sprites, dancing hand-in-hand in long grass around, making circles and cavorting in soft colours of the earth, red ochre jerkins and skirts made of petals.

Merry and innocent, in japes and jamborees, laughing like sleigh bells, hollowing out toadstools and coaxing will-o'-the-wisps to live in your lanterns.

Where else should you live but at the bottom of gardens? Magic spaces in between worlds that change at dawn and dusk into gleamings and gloamings. Fey fragile dwellings where walls are melting mists and curtains, crystal cobwebs, with gossamer garlands and a dewdrop looking glass.

Ethereal entities, mostly lost to us now, with our robust rationality and disdain for stories, shall we spot you if we crawl on our bellies, heart in mouth, quiet as cats? Or should we simply leave a note, Spike-like, under the smooth stone there by the stream, like we did as children?

Day Three Hundred and Three: Deck Chair

Midwinter dreaming today of lazy summer days, carefree barefoot lawn-lolling stretches and the flopping of straw hats over tired eyes. Siestas and catnaps, lulling mowing in the distance, in the heat, even the bees ambling in their bumbling. Newspapers over snoozing Dads, white hankies on grandfathers' bald heads, each corner knot no doubt a reminder of something.. no idea what and not likely to be coming to mind out here laying on the sleepy suburban striped sedan.

When they get up, you flap in the welcome wind like a thing possessed, a ship's flag in a gale, making me wonder if you long for the passenger liners you were made for, as we all yearn for our destinies, the salty sea spray, to live on deck, not decking.

Day Three Hundred and Four: Snowman

Out here in the blank canvas of snowman's land, you begin your life rolled like

icing or *Plasticine*, drawn the same way as a cartoon character, from two or three

spheres. One small globe on one large, like a crystalline cottage loaf, or an old

lady's mignon. Later the details will be added, but the foundations must first be

firmed by patting with ice-encrusted mittens and red-cold palms.

You come to life then, after searching, toing and froing and the loosing of

imagination on everyday objects, a spell cast on twigs and carrots, buttons and

coins. A genderless Frozen grin, the iceman cometh, full of stories, from Briggs

to Keaton, as many tales to tell as ways of melting, and the ending must always

be the same drippy disappearance, and your stay short. Make the most of your

beginning, middle and end, then, for the days do not lengthen for you and the

seasons must thaw into the ground.

Day Three Hundred and Five: Snowdrop

White as milk flower, soft snow bell ringing in the spring, such a delicate herald

at the end of winter, a tiny lily-like lolling head, more hardy than you seem.

Fairy petticoat, shimmering in the first gentle rays of sun, translucent beauty, a

sign of hope and change, like a pale tidal line in the flower beds, still half asleep,

drowsy nodding crown, a welcome whimsical wonder.

Day Three Hundred and Six: Nasturtium

Tropaeolum, trophy shields and helmets glinting golden in the sun, you were perhaps easy prey for the *conquistadors* who thought you a reflection of their headgear, and held you prisoner all the way from the Andes, locked in treasure chests swelled by the Atlantic, and who then stuck you in cottage gardens to be admired.

What a change of scene, like savannah lions finding themselves in a zoo, roots that laugh at 10,000 feet below them tucked into topsoil beds. You thrived of course, and spread, your cheerful Indian cress quickly winning botanical hearts and space to shine. You are hardy and bisexual and glorious and beautiful, no-one will cast aspersions on your name, your popularity gliding easily from one Elizabethan age to another.

Day Three Hundred and Seven: Icicles

Damocles' deadly daggers dangling by a transparent thread. You may fall and die hard, or you may gently melt, thawing into the thirsty ground below. Swords or ploughshares, we do not yet know.

Tubular bells worthy of an ice queen's palace, signs of deepest, burning cold, jagged frozen popsicles left hanging where the world has run off the edges and time has called a halt. Stopped motion, still rows of running water. One day you will be vapour, steam, droplets, for now you are dangerous dentistry, an avalanche of too too solid sharpness.

Day Three Hundred and Eight: Garden Path

Somewhere we should be wary of being led, as though beyond the flowerbeds were a strange place of uncertainties, a murky miasma where we can be tricked or despoiled of our innocence. But I say walk the garden path and be reassured by gravel and solidity, by concrete beneath your feet; bend down and smell the fragrant beds and breathe God's good air, however the way curves. For it is not when we are beyond knowing nor in the unexplored edges, but in the open places, by the trees in the centre, where the serpents most readily coil and hiss, soft sibilant syllables catching us off our guard, whispering wiles and doubts.

Day Three Hundred and Nine: Daffodil

Bright butter golden *hallelujah* heralds, the trumpet call for spring. Planted in rows, a floral fanfare blasting back the cold. Make way! Make way for the breaching bulbs, the cresting crocuses, the surfacing snowdrops!

Caerphilly daffadowndilly, one of Peter's leeks, Cymru's symbol cymbal, keep your head up proudly lest you narcissistically nod near water and fall for your own reflection, perfection too hard to keep up, you will only wilt and soon be broken hearted again. Beautiful claxon, sideways saffron cup and saucer, companion to Wordsworth's Windermere wanderings, zesty joyful megaphone, sing your song and birth new gladness in our weary wintered hearts.

Day Three Hundred and Ten: Wellingtons

I doubt the Iron Duke danced in puddles, or made mud pies for his troops, or sploshed his way to the shed to fetch Dad for dinner. Yet he left a legacy of little children feeling the give of bent boots, rubber rubbing into calves as they lean and crane over the pond, looking intently into jam jars and tiny nets, attention transfixed by alien life forms.

Looking with green eyes at the frog wellingtons, bright yellow ones with ducks on, the rainbow stripes, I feel a pang for a less colourful childhood, where my dark welly memories are of standing in the flooding drive realising the slow wetting of hosed feet through an undiscovered sole hole, and the same nasty wet awareness soaking in whilst stood in the plum orchard next to William the golden retriever, who clearly mistook my spindly legs for a tree.

Day Three Hundred and Eleven: Sprinkler

Like bad luck or good fortune, you suddenly vent, wet without warning, pouring cold water on your unsuspecting verge victims, giving them a soaking, the shock rallying tiny green blades shaking their fists at you until they reap the ripe verdancy and realise their thirst is assuaged.

Jumping jets: hot feet and playful toddlers run into your streams and screech or giggle as you struggle to maintain the serious business of timely irrigation, and then, after turning like a peacock's fan, you disappear in an instant, keeping to the background like all good back-groundkeepers.

Day Three Hundred and Twelve: Grafting

Knitting together root and scion, the skilled grafter whip stitches husband and wife together, or places budding in a cleft, or peels back bark to banana zip the new stock in. Such forced marriages bring forth quicker fruit, hardier lines, create new hybrids.

Does the interloper feel uncomfortable, unsure, or blissfully unaware of its adoption into the heart of another? Does the gardener wonder at his own deftness, at her ability to play God in splicing genes? Such lofty lordings were doubtless unknown by Leo, my unmet grandfather; the woodworker, the tree whisperer, the graftage genius who just wanted to feed his family. Carpenters' hands are planed rough, yet gentle; masterful with malleable myrtle, purposeful with pliant peaches, his ingrained knowledge working the meld, joining the tender tenons, binding the cross.

Day Three Hundred and Thirteen: Screens

Not silver, but golden woven willow warp and weft, or lashed bamboo raft, made for shade and privacy, not for films of fame or celluloid celebrities. A pointed partition, separating one use from another, a different kind of fence, protecting plants from the weather, sun or sleet perhaps, like a standing parasol.

No Windows here, no crashes or dumps, only the soft susurration of air moving through your matting, in and out, back and forth, not constantly checking for messages but only whispering, winding wafts of breeze.

Day Three Hundred and Fourteen: Goldcrest

Such a dainty, darting visitor, as welcome a sight as ever there was, hopping to-and-fro on the rose bush, pecking at peeking buds or ambling aphids, a strange shaped dinner plate for sure. Golden green jacket and striped sleeves, that one dashing streak of butter on your head, as though you had cheekily stood a moment under the drip of God's paintbrush and come away with a royal crown.

You are, in any case, part of heaven's treasure trove, and we who search in the mouths of every fish for a tax haven might miss this warbling, flighty Fort Knox if we take our eyes off the garden and focus too hard on the empty piggy bank inside.

Day Three Hundred and Fifteen: Afternoon Tea

Tiffin time, silver pots and sugar bowls, table and chairs laid out on the lawn. A leftover from colonial customs, perhaps, when the houseboy poured from Wedgwood held in bemused white kid fingers, wondering at the strange ways of the rich and pale. Now, thank God, we all sit at the same table, gloves off and manners left free and easy, the laughter rolling in waves and the crumbs landing wherever they please in the grass, to feed opportunistic Samaritan sparrows.

Cucumber sandwiches cut free from their crusts, handbags dangling from chair backs, cream spilling from chocolate éclairs, the relaxation is palpable and a butter knife slides through scones, not tension, the etiquette police say move along, nothing to see here, and we cast our cares and calorie counters to the wind and shake our napkins white and free, like sails in the afternoon air.

Day Three Hundred and Sixteen: Trug

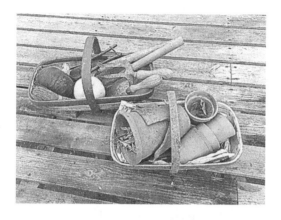

Carried by Georgian ladies in organza, organising herbs and cutting lavender to dry, finding the choicest roses to cut for mama's boudoir whilst the servants do the real gardening and the maids nurse their wind-whipped chillblains. Austen's heroines daintily balance you upon lace-kissed arms as they whisper sisterly confidences and make beau jests.

A short, ugly name for a regency prop and a bringer-in of bounty, a carrier of aroma and kitchen garden goodness. A cornucopia full of different things daily, a diligent worker, content to always be the container and never the treasure, like many a humble thing, close to the ground.

Photograph by Gill Fuller, used with permission.

Day Three Hundred and Seventeen: Iris

Ragged rainbow flower, royal purple velvet cloak with golden lining, your beauty is beguiling and dramatic, drawing the eye and the admiration of the beholder: iris locked on iris, namesakes and bright iridescence held in common with a gaze.

Bright sparkling wit, sharp as a tack, the ex-Wren who also shares your name and conversation over cups of tea with me in the church hall. All synapses firing, memories flowing unabated, un-dulled by decades disappeared. I shall always think of her when I see your navy flags, your unfading, deeply saturated colour, your life in abundance.

Day Three Hundred and Eighteen: Love-in-a-mist

Syrian Nigella, beautiful sky-blue buttercup surrounded by cloudy bracts, a layered petticoat of cottage garden loveliness. A ragged lady perhaps, but despite being around from one Elizabethan age to another, not showing your own. When you do go to seed, you change like Miss Jekyll into Mrs Hyde, sunsetting from blue to pink, becoming a space age capsule, or a swollen belly of new life.

Love is always cloudy, unsure, surrounded by spikes, a crown of thorns perhaps, difficult to pin down, the colours and shapes ever changing, like our married bodies and our hearts.

Day Three Hundred and Nineteen: Kneeler

Weeding or praying, each grounded in good faith, humility the key and proximity to the dust we came from a blessing that keeps pride in check as we tend to flower beds or souls, contemplating the beauty before us. Support for the joints, a cushioning between worlds of flesh and soil, an upholding that keeps us just above hard, stony ground and able to lean into the work set at hand.

A soft spongy helpmate, the best kind, that yields yet sits firm and does not crack under our weight but moulds to our shape without judging it. A cheerful, easy going companion for this most sacred task, of delving into the deep dirt, God's own earth.

Day Three Hundred and Twenty: Peacock

Mesmerising moving fan, swishing back and forth coquettishly and with brazen purpose, staring out at all your admirers with your own made-up eyes. Avian ego over-spilling into Indian jewelled colours and a crowned head, kohled cold-blooded bird, winning our hypnotised hearts before we know you well enough, ere we hear your raucous call and spellbound, mistake it for a love song.

Day Three Hundred and Twenty-One: Manure

The dwelling place of the desperate, we the denizens of the dung heap, forced to listen to friends telling us to pull ourselves out, dust ourselves off, that we should ignore the crap that has fallen on us from a great height, or else accept that this is our just desserts, curse God and die. But they don't understand, don't feel the weight of the woe and the weeping sores that steal our energy and sap our strength and leave us stranded here. There is only one encounter that can release us from this *gehenna*.

Years later, we can look back and see that the muck raked over us, the fertilizer that fell in flurries, the deep dirt that held us in a half-nelson all that time, were layers of life-giving nutrients. That now we have risen and bloomed, we are like roaring red roses, lifted up by growth above the steaming smells and released into being ourselves, far the stronger and brighter for the manure heaped around our roots.

Day Three Hundred and Twenty-Two: Grey Squirrel

Wolfish coat and foxy tail, you brush and dash across the lawn, your deep dark eyes taking everything in, two little oceans of seeing. Your twitching food detector working overtime by the bird table; your ingenuity and crafty rodent claws defeating any fiendish boundaries.

I am rather in awe of you if I may admit it here amongst furry friends. You take on any impossible mission, climbing upside down along twine with acrobatic ease, and can still remember where you buried last year's stash of treasure, whereas I can't even find my glasses half the time, even when they are perched, like you on this rock, atop my own head.

Day Three Hundred and Twenty-Three: Ice

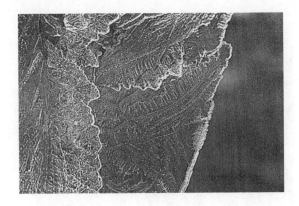

Freezing wind, dropped degrees, callous cold, all cause you to stop in your tracks. A temperature time-out whilst you regroup in crystals and take stock, hold still. So used to moving, momentum, onwards and upwards, does it feel frustrating, this becoming a standing surface? Ducks skating on you, the world going about its business whilst you feel locked down, mute, immobile, in burning limbo.

Yet the thaw will come, the softening sound of spring dripping into your soul, the start of sunrays nudging you gently. You are tentative like the Tin Man's oiled jaw, ripples on the pond beginning again and reaching out to melt your oh too solid flesh. Then you will feel the joy of regaining what was lost and find the landscape changed beneath you, rocks cracked and tiny valleys formed, surprised by your stationary strength, now you can let go and flow.

Day Three Hundred and Twenty-Four: Crocus

Spring bravehearts, lavender Labradors, bounding out of the ground to chase

after sunlight before anyone else is ready, opening up to the bright, oh so

welcome shafts of warmth that chase away winter, hitting your readied solar

panelled petals and colouring your stamens saffron gold. We had forgotten where

the treasure was buried, all these long dark days, but now we see.

Day Three Hundred and Twenty-Five: Frogspawn

Little black seeds, commas in jelly, waiting *en masse* for the water to warm a little, growing inside shell-less eggs, your larder surrounding you, jailor and protector, until you are big enough to fend for yourselves.

We too, must be nourished and take our time to mature. The deep will seem large enough when we find release, and none of us should be in too much of a hurry. If the jam jars and the herons come, then we shall simply pass through this world more quickly, but I secretly hope that each and every one of you will make it, becoming darling hoppy froglets, pinging in the grass and standing on my hand, having not yet learnt to be anything but unafraid.

Photograph by Chris Wicks, used with permission.

Day Three Hundred and Twenty-Six: Weather Vane

More accurate than the Met Office, who attempt to police the weather, herding it

into isobars, you can tell us where the wind blows and where it's going to, by

simply pointing, Dylan-like, to the answer.

You may be a plastic windmill perched on a fence, only sure of one thing, or you

may be a cast iron cockerel bolted to the pinnacle of a pagoda, gazing over grand

lawns, but still you take pride in your position, bringer of good tidings or bad,

you have us reaching for the umbrella, the Macintosh or the parasol and tutting at

the sky Britishly, whilst secretly hoping the thunder gods will not strike us down

for our insolence.

Day Three Hundred and Twenty-Seven: Duckweed

Simplest plant with the smallest known flower, a pond covering meniscus of pure green, a chlorophyll carpet spread across the water. Food for fowl, dinner for ducks, minute lilypads layering the lake. Water clover, bayroot basil, a being that decided to devolve back into primordial pea-soup. I feel that hankering myself sometimes, (mostly in the presence of politicians) as in Vonnegut's imaginings, a retreat from progress into quiet simplicity, a yearning to float on still waters, rafting gently through the days, messing about on the river, soaking up the sun and spreading out across the surface of life aquatic.

Day Three Hundred and Twenty-Eight: Greater Spotted Woodpecker

Not spotted as often as your name would suggest, yet your racketeering reaches for miles as you jackhammer with your beak into the heartwood and make your home there. A woody hollow, a mosh pit for headbangers from whence you fly to our bird tables and suet in nets.

An old rocker, swaying back and forth, two toes forward, two back, expert cramponed climber, resting on your coat-tails as you work. A newspaper bird, black and white and red all over, your cardinal colours surprise for one so seldom seen, but often heard.

Day Three Hundred and Twenty-Nine: Dog

Faithful fluffy friend, great lolling tongue and paws like saucers, or tiny lap dog chasing reindeer with difficulty, named after saints and tonsured at the grooming parlour, clipped and collared, yet loving and loyal.

I wonder how we ever dared abuse such absolute trust; shortening, stretching, aggressing, harnessing, docking, playing with pedigrees. Let us instead allow you to spread, roll, run madly after sticks, leap into lakes and come pelting back to shake your muddy finds all over us. Let us laugh together and tussle with towels, de-squeak rubber ducks and drip drool generously, making a mongrel mess and having your day - charging through the crash barriers at Crufts, tearing a trail through toppling trophies.

Day Three Hundred and Thirty: Vine

Outside of you, cut off on my own, I can do nothing. One leaf, one steam, one flower, one grape, none of these alone can weave along a string, wind along a trellis, hold the sun's gaze, bloom gloriously, fruit fulsomely, bunch into the vintner's delight. No, this is a team game, a body of many parts, all conjoined and co-operating, and the lifeblood all yours, given for us.

Those apart will falter, fall to the ground, look on with jealous misunderstanding, and be fit only for mulch. But even then, there may be a hope of rootish reconciliation, and a rebirth into nutrients that may yet be lifted on high as one of the glory-reflecting, wrath-deflecting grapes.

Day Three Hundred and Thirty-One: Laurel

Evergreen crown, prize-winning plant, encircler of champion heads and noble brows, perhaps you adorned Caesar's cranium whilst another, more thorny wreath graced a less grand man, emperor only of eternity.

Waxing lyrical, deep shade speaking of abundant life all year around, you tell tales of treasure that never fades or falls.

Dancing with Babe and singing of Blue Ridge Mountains in every possible register, for me you will always be associated with belly laughs and thumbs that light cigars.

Day Three Hundred and Thirty-Two: Myrtle

A myriad of Myrtles, some Australian, some South American, gorgeous pinks and whites, here raspberry candyfloss waving atop the bushes. Our own Myrtle Maclagan scoring the first century in women's test cricket against the Aussies, with such a name, a double blow, like being hit with one's own bat, the soft thunk of leather on willow.

A strong feminine independence, name of many flappers, poets and athletes, a beauty, a vibrance, a depth of colour that sings, (no moaners here) a cerise tide of achievement, a name and flower that should make a Great Gatsby graceful comeback, knocking Chelsea and Kayleigh effortlessly for six.

Day Three Hundred and Thirty-Three: Rosehip

Haws in Hilda Hughes' wartime syrup, a tonic, carrier of vitamin C, a pick-me-up, in colour and cordial, Hungarian *palinka*, Slovenian *cockta*, soothing arthritic joints, making hips and cheeks rosy again.

Red nub of a fruit, a concentrated rose berry with more inside, waiting to bloom. A bud held tight by a seeded fist and dissuaded to travel by tough skin and itching powder hairs, reluctant to leave home, stuck fast to the bush, this crimson apple will not fall far from the tree.

Day Three Hundred and Thirty-Four: Bay leaf

Shady herb, dark greenly delicious, aromatic shielded shape, wide and brim-full of flavour. Firstly fragrant and then, torn from the tree, left to dry and desiccate, seasoned before seasoning, releasing taste into stews and soups, in Mediterranean tureens.

The bay base for myrcene, merciful release into pungent perfumes, spicy, deep tones, natural incense sensed by Grecian noses many moons ago. Shall our scent too drift across decades, our tang and essence increasing after death like yours, remaining alive in memory and story, in history and tale? Or does fragrance fade like an old sepia photograph, left too long in an album, barely there, untraceable faces, lost lines.

Day Three Hundred and Thirty-Five: Weasel

Dashing in and out of the undergrowth, quick as a whip, light as a duckling, not here to stay but only a raider of the lost bird's nest, or maybe to hitch a ride on a passing woodpecker! Japanese *yokai*, shapeshifting spirit, or words that undermine themselves, like a burrowing creature disappearing into a hole, retreating from its own meaning.

Slick enemies of Mr Toad, poo-pooing his powered caravan and setting yourselves up in the ancestral hall. Never to be underestimated, ingenious not ingenuous, soft and silky as living stockings, you should have watch fobs and spats, and tip your bowlers forward like George Cole as you saunter along.

Day Three Hundred and Thirty-Six: Primrose

First flower, Eve of the garden, prima donna in pale, margarine yellow with a buttery centre, an open palm held out to the patter of early rains, cupping primrose promise, ushering in the spring season, a feast of blooming just beginning.

I remember the thrill of seeking out your glory in woodland glades as a child, the coming upon, around a corner, your golden treasure, laid out shyly like constellations in patches of sage sky on your cabbage-like leaves, pin-eyed and thrum-eyed stargazers, delicate and divine.

Day Three Hundred and Thirty-Seven: Vole

Bank, field or water, you range around, messing about on the river or burrowing below the ground to devour bulbs and roots. Small, brown and furry, rounder than the mice you are mistaken for. You live such a short time, but are busy every second. Voles the proles, the lower echelons, last in the food chain, carried off by hawks and buzzards, owls and foxes, oppressed down in the dirt yet ever cheerful, cheeks full, hardly ever ratty, a sweet friendly face to meet with.

Always it seems the ones below stairs that keep everyone else going are the least offensive, most delightful; working hard with the rest of nature balancing on your soft shoulders.

Photograph by Jeannie Kendall, used with permission.

Day Three Hundred and Thirty-Eight: Water Feature

Sight and sound of the water falling, a softly liquid noise that takes us, via closed eye day dreaming to the streams we played in as children, or maybe to the sonorous amniotic fluidity before that. Squealing at the spotting of tiny fishes round our toes, minnows meandering, the coolness of barefooted splashing and the roundness of stones curled into the arches of our feet.

Day Three Hundred and Thirty-Nine: Sage

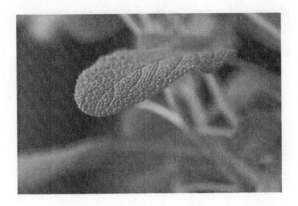

Soft grey-green healing leaves, your undersides crowned with white wisdom, sage the saviour, bringing balm to our wounds and holding the plague at bay with your three thief fraternity, gazing at the stars with your fellow magi.

Championed by Charlemagne, ever warding off evil, you are plentiful in the cloisters and your very name echoes monastery stores and the keeping of knowledge.

To me you will always speak of the hidden depths in feline familiars' eyes; the wise green mossy orbs blinking kisses and rolling with purrs, the furry friends both present and much missed.

Three Hundred and Forty: Cucumber

Watery truncheon, butt of the joke, strange, alien green cylinder; your seeds running through you like Brighton in rock, spread out like soft stars in a pale mint sky. Staple for Lady Bracknell's sawn-off "sarndwidges", crusts flung to the garden birds or saved for a summer pudding in which they cannot give offence with their rough edges.

Cold frame sausages, greenhouse torpedoes, our salads would be lifeless sans your cross-sectioned circles, cheery cubes, racing green refreshment, establishment English eating.

Day Three Hundred and Forty-One: Patio

Skating rink for snails, roofless room readied for repasts, plastic furniture awaiting summer squash in beakers and the placing of paper plates loaded with cheese rolls and crisps that drift off in the wind, a surprise snack for a sparrow.

Concrete slabs, heavy and solid, a floor reliably permanent with parking for bicycle and barbecue, and yet, left untended, the dandelions will force their way up through the sandy gaps and cracked joins, the tree roots and soaked soil will heave their shoulders a little here and there till the edges become uneven, the corners lifted, waiting to trip us up, like everything that seems immutable and eternal, nature reclaiming all things.

Day Three Hundred and Forty-two: Fox

Fantastique Monsieur Reynard, Vive Madame Vixen, here we are honoured and glad to catch glimpses of such graceful garden visitors, day or night, a flash of elegant red on green, a fleet-footed rush of rust-coloured fur dashing past, and, thank God, no hounding here.

Mesmerising emerald eyes one end and a perfectly balanced brush the other, held out straight as you dart by or stand statue still, meeting our gaze and turning us to stone, caught in the headlights of awe, wild wonder keeping us at bay.

Day Three Hundred and Forty-three: Humming Bird Hawkmoth

Mistaken for your namesake more often than you care to think about, tiny avian imitator with your taste for deep nectar, bird brain hovering near honeysuckle and buzzing over buddleia.

How you thrum and seem to be alight, the fire no doubt begun by rubbing your two wings together, or maybe by the spell *Macroglossum Stellatarum*, orange flames against the blue sky, a phoenix risen from the bedstraw that your caterpillars turned to gold.

Day Three Hundred and Forty-Four: Badger

Set in your ways, a bumbling, low down monochrome misfit, sanguine stripes on your friendly face. Squinting in the daylight, more alive at dusk and dawn, a nightcrawler seeking sluggish prey, we love you as Brock and Badger, friend to Mole and Ratty, looking disdainfully down your *pince-nez* at the boisterousness of toads.

A testament to the cruelty of humankind, who could blame you and cull you, bait you and run you down, but also to the beauty of black and white, when they deign to live together, quietly in the secret copses and the hidden dens of middle England. Here is where I know you best, *ssh*ing in hides, watching the wise grey heads lift to sniff the air, the bustling stumpy tail just visible in the half-light. Gentlefolk of the glade, crossing our garden paths only as they intersect with your ancient byways and highways, Grahame's treasured sage.

Photograph by Jeannie Kendall, used with permission.

Day Three Hundred and Forty-Five: Black-eyed Susan

Maryland's motif, a teepee built with balm in mind by the *Objiwa* people, a post held up high for the healing of snake bites, a vine against venom, a pretty poultice maker.

Are you *Golden Jerusalem*, a shining of temple treasures and Torah scrolls, or a victim of domestic violence, the aggro of a bruise hidden in plain sight, black in yellow, like Van Gogh's dying sunflowers, leaving all who see you stunned and powerless, unaware of your true worth?

Day Three Hundred and Forty-Six: Pea

Pea-soupers from my parents' childhood trips to London, a foggy fug of gaseous green. Owls and pussy-cats' top choice of keel colour, floating out to far-flung lands. The noise that makes us all put fingers in our cheeks, parodying young Patsy, the popping open of God's polythene, sugar-snap release of freshness.

The likeness of each one, round with a tiny nubbed nose, bullet-hard till boiled, and the powerful aroma of nature's newness, a little green unzipped slipper, a crib of cosy spheres, a line of tiny planets, some with a wriggly visitor that would make me squeal and drop the pod when shelling you with my Dad, sat in the back garden under the Damson tree, relaxed-ly busy, calmly occupied, bowls before us, filling nicely, dinner freshly picked, goodness gathered.

Day Three Hundred and Forty-Seven: Hand Rail

My stationary stair-lift, a helping hand, the cool curved surface under my palm feels strong and upholds me as I attempt the everyday for most, an Everest for M.E. We all need someone to lean on, a shoulder to support us on the climb, up or down, a focus point, a straight line to guide us.

Perhaps you look incongruous, rust-resistant black paint against the daisy-speckled lawn, as if part of the Titanic landed by my steps. But disability aids are never built for beauty and blatantly shout their presence. "Do you need help? Here I am, I will help you stand, I will let you move, I will be here!" If only people were as steadfast, or so ready to remain, like the everlasting, underlying arms of heaven.

Day Three Hundred and Forty-Eight: Ladder

Stairway less grand than Jacob's but still a way to higher things, a raising up and

a steadying, feet firmly in the soil and held against a tree trunk or a wall.

Steadfast colleague for roofers, loppers and climbers, you may be relied upon for

support and for firm footholds. Not for the hooves of biblical mountain gazelles

perhaps, but for trainers and wellington boots. Companion in working, mending,

pruning and tiling, helper in the wrestling we do with nature and its persistent

growth and interference, you give us the stilts to see a new perspective and a

taste for the heights, or a longing for the ground. Either way we find out where

we belong and relish the knowing.

Later, when the mugs of tea are handed out, rungs on their side become railings

for wallflowers to peep through and ask whether it is all over.

Day Three Hundred and Forty-Nine: Picnic Table

Might we, one day, see a stone fox and his friends come to life, mid-toast, at your seated place? Not out of place in Narnia, though of course no-one there seems in need of back support, eyeing you with the dread of later pain as I do in this, more fallen world. To others, you are a symbol of summer al fresco food, of joyful banter and the squashing up of thighs, the rustle of cotton sliding along against the grain to fit everyone in the feasting halls.

Lawn lunching half-way, not curled up on the ground, made anxious by ants, but still wasp-watching, Tupperware tucking, measuring the heaviness of the skies with grabbed glances, just in case. Picnics the province of Mad dogs and Englishmen in a place where sandwiches get sodden or skins scorched, and little in between. A lunching limbo land, set at the bottom of the garden, as if distance from civilisation might tame the errant weather.

Day Three Hundred and Fifty: Delphiniums

Striving for the sky, standing tall on tip-roots wanting to touch blue to blue. Who

am I to dash your Michelangelo hopes and say you will never make it? Perhaps

the bottle-nose swimmer who holds your nectar longs to dive into those far

above heavenly oceans?

So beautiful, so deadly, poisoned petals still favoured by cottage gardeners

everywhere, tolerant for the sake of your flowered towers and reaching blooms.

You may be toxic, but by golly you know how to break up an expanse of wall,

and the dot moths and small angled shades are happy to have their nursery here,

lulled by larkspur lullabies.

Day Three Hundred and Fifty-One: Rabbit

Flopsy, Mopsy and Cottontail will stay here in the garden, neatly dressed in pinafores, whilst Peter goes on an allotment raid. Bigwig and Hazel might be prepared to join him, but Fiver will sit and go all mystical on us, those big brown dreamy eyes seeing as much closed as open.

Such mottled marvellous multiplying variety, no two exactly alike, despite their rate of reproduction, individual works of art, just as we are. "Princes with a thousand enemies", nibblers of lawn, chewers of carrots, enquiring about the Doctor's day and missing left turns at Albuquerque, inspiring soulful songs and epic tales, all before lolloping back by teatime, mysteriously laden with vegetables and dandelion leaves. Mr MacGregor exclaiming "Were Rabbit!" and answered by a giggling Boston Bunny, well hidden in the hedgerow, "There, rabbit!"

Day Three Hundred and Fifty-Two: Jay

Garrulous (*Glandarius*) but hard to spot, except perhaps that splash of white tail flashing as you dart between two trees, painting a line for a twitcher's hammock.

Mostly you are aware of your family crest, crowing as you screech; but in autumn you have an identity crisis and imagine you are a squirrel, gathering acorns and burying them like tawny treasure.

Your dusky pink body and dark blue wing stripes fascinated me as a child, when suburbia still backed onto woodland in places and people let forests flourish. When we knew that glimpses of such grandness were things to be grateful for, and that the edges and betweens of our worlds should be maintained.

Day Three Hundred and Fifty-Three: Lichen

An unnoticed miracle, a marriage between fungus and algae that defies all logic and creates a soulful symbiosis subsisting on sunlight and living on (sometimes in) pure air.

Frilly flakes and rusting ripples, resting on rocks, growing on gravestones, beautifying branches, sitting gently, not rooted, stealing nothing but space; still, silent silver that shines in the sunlight; overlooked ecosystems that you won't see on *Survival*; patches of precious metal attached to surfaces; fascinating fronded undramatic couples, constant and loving, the one barely knowing where the other begins, never marking their frontiers.

Day Three Hundred and Fifty-Four: Cuckoo

Striped spring summoner, clock-dwelling feathered fiend, a calling card left to devour the labour of others. Reared changeling, how do you then know who to become, when you fly the borrowed nest, confused sparrows waving you goodbye, whilst the one who should have fledged lies mouldering below?

The season you usher in is full of life and burgeoning hope, but so much death must make room for its greedy green gushing. For spring is a time of anger too, when the losses feel keener. Bare branches minister to a shared grief, but blossom seems to defy our misery, that heartbreak that we may not be yet ready to take from our breast.

And yet, your confident, cooing call, two notes only, singing your own name, heralds a tidal change that must come, overriding our emotions and pronouncing movement, resurrection, newness, even for those who are not yet ready.

Photograph by Stephen Root, used with permission.

Day Three Hundred and Fifty-Five: Stump

Deadwood city, a "hive of scum and villainy," full of beetle larvae and woodlice, scurrying ants running to and from the nursery, precious cargo in arms. In nature, death is always full of life, the one giving way to the other, like mulch feeds green shoots, nutrients pouring themselves out into new forms.

Somewhere flat to stop and mull these things, a Franciscan seat for welcoming sister death and brother woodworm, a pondering platform for the posteriors of students of philosophy and other dreamers. And even this may birth new life, some world-changing deep thought that never knew a synapse, full of promise, like the stump of Jesse bringing forth the saviour of the world.

Day Three Hundred and Fifty-Six: Pots

Cracked or broken, pouring stagnant water, roots trailing, last year's overgrown gone-to-seed plants cascading over your lip, blown bulbs half in and half out of the exhausted soil. Tubs and pots easily transformed by compost, secateurs and a watering can into a new thing, fresh mercies abounding, fissures mended with the gold of buttercups or primroses, like natural *kintsugi*. Soon the growth of spring will be making your cup overflow with blooms and the straggly, wooded stems and soggy seeds will be a distant memory, at least until next year.

Day Three Hundred and Fifty-Seven: Rat

Rumblings in the compost heap, dashings across the lawn, you must not give the game away so easily. For such visibility will lead to the speaking of the word, "vermin" and this means "pest-control" is only three syllables away. And it may sound clinical and clean, but for you it may bring poison, gnashing terriers or metal traps. So stay quiet and unseen as Victorian children, noiseless as asylum seekers.

Keep out of sight and mind. Find your way into pet shops where you become magically friendly and hygienic, and where your delightful intelligence transforms into skilful and imaginative play: in freedom it will remain guile and cunning. Spin your cv from straw to gold, from conniving to cuddly, from plague carriers to *Pets"R"Us*.

Either that, or run, fast and free, dive into the detritus we leave everywhere, unacknowledged, dig deep, and keep us in the dark.

Day Three Hundred and Fifty-Eight: Magnolia

Magnificent even in bud, shrugging your pink shoulders out of furry boleros, nothing prepares us for the chorus of colour that is coming. Fabulousness unfurling into blossomed beauty, out-of-its-shell pink, pale porcelain petals.

The display will last only a fortnight or so, but will imprint itself so deeply on our memories, like an Ang Lee film, that we will eagerly await next year's showing, recalling the angelic vision of those wonderful curved wings every time we look at the bare branches.

Day Three Hundred and Fifty-Nine: Peach

Luscious and delicious, soft and golden, heavy, heavenly fruit that feels wicked, juices running down our chins. Late summer bounty, your cherubic baby-bottom shape that fits in our hands, cheeks blushing with goodness; innocence leading, as it does inevitably, to experience. Taste and see that it is good.

Unsceptred orb, you are tender and your blossom palest pretty. You bruise so easily and yet left to grow to full potential, you can cross an ocean and defeat sharks with your wonderful roundness (and the help of seagulls) helmed by a small Dahl-ing boy.

I wonder if the stone-grown tree my Dad planted as a child has remained intact, or if it exists now only in his memory and my heard knowing. If he returned to that garden now, would the tree be so glad that it would cover itself in welcoming petals, or would the selfish giant of time have whisked it away?

Day Three Hundred and Sixty: Bird Table

Gathering place, where feathery friends flock together, stocking up on sunflower seeds or taking off with tired crusts, depending on the bounty of the day. A place for me to scatter my offerings and see if anyone will come to glean the goodness. A giving table, an altar of altruism, a laying down of my words in hopes of new arrivals.

If you give me in return a glimpse of new colours, an acrobatic display, a lifting of the heart, a kernel of glee, a smattering of song, then I am happy. Feed well, feel free to return for more, show me your flights of freedom.

Day Three Hundred and Sixty-One: Cowslip

Not the first flower, *primula veris*, but the first to sound spring by klaxon, flaxen loudhailers all in a circle, blasting out a trumpet fanfare. A reminder that butter grows out of manured fields and that where there's muck there's brass; shiny golden treasure boldly sticking up all over the meadow like unruly tufts of hair.

When small, I wondered at the idea of cattle wearing petticoats, and now I see perhaps these are the buckles that might decorate their hooves, or perhaps fairy cups holding nectar wine. Better yet, Peter's keys, dropped in a field, so that anyone, anywhere, even at the bottom of a garden where you've snuck in through a hedge, might encounter the means to open heaven's gates.

Day Three Hundred and Sixty-Two: Gnomes

Eerily cheery figurines, disturbingly happy about fishing in concrete or watering non-existent plants, you crop up in circles and we hesitate in your presence, one wellington in the air, feeling like we should cough or maybe even knock. Is it your garden or ours?

Brightly jerkin-ed, bell-hatted, tubby and bearded, are there any lady gnomes? And where do you go at night, I wonder? Do you wander as I suspect, to the local faerie hostelry? And if not, how do you maintain that magnificent beer belly and the rosy cheeks of excess? Are you our idea of idyll, idle idols: lolling about and taking your time, never uneasy or depressed, anxious or grumpy (those are dwarves), just laughing at some joke of the cosmic gardener that we were never let in on?

Day Three Hundred and Sixty-Three: Greenhouse

Teamed now with gases and effect, yet in my day you were a forbidden fortress. No ball games nearby lest there were breakages, and standing in the focussed heat if allowed inside to look at (do not touch!) the ripening tomatoes, made me feel uncomfortable, like in the car on the way to a summer holiday, desperate to wind the windows down, thighs sticking to the red plastic interior of our Austin Maxi.

Dangerous too, for I didn't see a woman in a greenhouse till I was past twenty. I wondered if they might faint away or feel like an ant underneath a magnifying glass. I breathed in the compost smell, the peaty growbag aroma, but the whole place felt unnatural, too hurried, bent on success. A little dank too, and not glamorous like Kew's Crystal Palace, seen on Blue Peter, spaciously filled with orchids and tropical trees, not listless seedlings, piles of terracotta coloured plastic pots, and small girls trying to work out the mysteries of Dad.

Day Three Hundred and Sixty-Four: Barn Owl

Moon-faced marvel, Athena of the night skies, ghostly hooter and swooping spectre, such pale and wondrous beauty! Winged wisdom, silver softness with a tinge of burnished bronze. You bury your blessèd head in barns, roosting on rafters, a finder of warm and cosy corners despite your ethereal shimmer, a home bird night owl, one who graces us like an avian moonbeam, and yet who also conjures the image of Plop, who was afraid of the dark.

Photograph by Kevin Thornhill, used with permission.

Day Three Hundred and Sixty-Five: Sunset

The warmest colours sink with you: rivulets of pink, gold and red, no cloud here lined with silver; instead the nectarine hues of juice running down the face of the heavens; molten nuggets swirling in their channels. A time to sit and ponder, as the coolness of evening revisits the garden, a betweening in which to wander and wonder in holy awe.

Death of day, as the yolk slips silently behind the curve of the earth and into the space filled by faith alone. Yet here also the birthing of a new season of dawning dark, of sacred sleepy silence, seeping into the sky like ink in water.

Awake, north wind,
and come, south wind!
Blow on my garden,
that its fragrance may
spread everywhere.
Let my beloved come into
his garden
and taste its choice fruits.

Song of Songs 4:16 NIV

Whale Song: Choosing Life with Jonah
A semi-autobiographical Bible Study

Positive Sisterhood
A handbook for the edification of Christian women

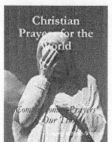

Christian Prayers for the World
A free e-book of prayers

About the Author

Keren Dibbens-Wyatt is a contemplative in the Christian tradition with a passion for prayer and creativity. She writes to encourage others into knowing the Lord more intimately as well as to share the poetic ponderings of her heart. A Christian for over 30 years, Keren has been answering a call into a deep prayer relationship for half that time, practising centring prayer and contemplation daily. She is no stranger to difficulties as she has had disabling M.E. for two decades, often being housebound or using a wheelchair.

Keren lives in Kent, "The Garden of England," with her poet husband and their slightly deranged black and white cat. She writes prayers, poetry, blogs, theology, prose-poems, short stories for adults and fiction for older children. She writes regularly for Godspace (the blog of Mustard Seed Associates) and guest posts on spiritual matters for other Christian sites. She has recently discovered a talent for painting in pastels which she enjoys immensely, and other interests when she has the energy include reading, enjoying nature, photography and crocheting things that inevitably come out wonky.

You can connect with Keren at her website **www.kerendibbenswyatt.com**

#0063 - 040417 - C0 - 210/148/21 - PB - DID1804683